OECD *Economic Surveys*
Electronic Books

The OECD, recognising the strategic role of electronic publishing, will be issuing the OECD *Economic Surveys*, both for the Member countries and for countries of Central and Eastern Europe covered by the Organisation's Centre for Co-operation with Economies in Transition, as electronic books with effect from the 1994/1995 series -- incorporating the text, tables and figures of the printed version. The information will appear on screen in an identical format, including the use of colour in graphs.

The electronic book, which retains the quality and readability of the printed version throughout, will enable readers to take advantage of the new tools that the ACROBAT software (included on the diskette) provides by offering the following benefits:

- ❑ User-friendly and intuitive interface
- ❑ Comprehensive index for rapid text retrieval, including a table of contents, as well as a list of numbered tables and figures
- ❑ Rapid browse and search facilities
- ❑ Zoom facility for magnifying graphics or for increasing page size for easy readability
- ❑ Cut and paste capabilities
- ❑ Printing facility
- ❑ Reduced volume for easy filing/portability

Working environment: DOS, Windows or Macintosh.

Subscription:	FF 1 800	US$317	£200	DM 545
Single issue:	FF 130	US$24	£14	DM 40

Complete 1994/1995 series on CD-ROM:

	FF 2 000	US$365	£220	DM 600

Please send your order to OECD Electronic Editions or, preferably, to the Centre or bookshop with whom you placed your initial order for this Economic Survey.

OECD
ECONOMIC
SURVEYS

1994-1995

JAPAN

ORGANISATION FOR ECONOMIC CO-OPERATION AND DEVELOPMENT

ORGANISATION FOR ECONOMIC CO-OPERATION AND DEVELOPMENT

Pursuant to Article 1 of the Convention signed in Paris on 14th December 1960, and which came into force on 30th September 1961, the Organisation for Economic Co-operation and Development (OECD) shall promote policies designed:

— to achieve the highest sustainable economic growth and employment and a rising standard of living in Member countries, while maintaining financial stability, and thus to contribute to the development of the world economy;

— to contribute to sound economic expansion in Member as well as non-member countries in the process of economic development; and

— to contribute to the expansion of world trade on a multilateral, non-discriminatory basis in accordance with international obligations.

The original Member countries of the OECD are Austria, Belgium, Canada, Denmark, France, Germany, Greece, Iceland, Ireland, Italy, Luxembourg, the Netherlands, Norway, Portugal, Spain, Sweden, Switzerland, Turkey, the United Kingdom and the United States. The following countries became Members subsequently through accession at the dates indicated hereafter: Japan (28th April 1964), Finland (28th January 1969), Australia (7th June 1971), New Zealand (29th May 1973) and Mexico (18th May 1994). The Commission of the European Communities takes part in the work of the OECD (Article 13 of the OECD Convention).

Publié également en français.

Table of contents

Tables

Figures

BASIC STATISTICS OF JAPAN

THE LAND

Area (1 000 sq. km)	377.8	Major cities, October 1994 estimate (10 000 inhabitants):	
Cultivated agricultural land (1 000 sq. km, 1992)	51.7	Tokyo (23 wards)	802
Forest (1 000 sq. km, 1992)	252.1	Yokohama	330
Densely inhabited districts[1] (1 000 sq. km, 1990)	11.7	Osaka	258
		Nagoya	215
		Sapporo	175
		Kobe	152
		Kyoto	145

THE PEOPLE

Population, October 1994 estimate (1 000)	125 034	Labour force in per cent of total population,	
Number of persons per sq. km in 1994	330	October 1994	53.1
Percentage of population living in densely		Percentage distribution of employed persons, 1994:	
inhabited district in 1990[1]	63.2	Agriculture and forestry	5.3
Net annual rate of population increase (1985-1994)	0.4	Manufacturing	23.2
		Service	23.9
		Other	47.6

PRODUCTION

Gross domestic product in 1994 (billion yen)	469 149	Growth of real gross fixed investment, 1981-1994	
Growth of real GDP, 1981-1994 average		average (annual rate, per cent)	3.6
(annual rate, per cent)	3.1	Net domestic product of agriculture, forestry and	
Gross fixed investment in 1994 (per cent of GDP)	28.6	fishery, at market prices, in 1993 (billion yen)	8 340
		Growth of production in manufacturing 1981-1994	
		(annual rate, per cent)	2.1

THE GOVERNMENT

		House of Representatives	House of Councillors
Public consumption in 1994 (in per cent of GDP)	9.8	Composition of Parliament, October 1995:	
Current public revenue in 1993 (in per cent of GDP)	32.9	Liberal Democratic Party	210	112
Government employees in per cent of total employment, 1994	8.4	New Frontier Party	169	–
		Heiseikai	–	69
Outstanding long-term national bonds in per cent of GDP (FY 1994)	43.1	Socialist Party	64	38
		Sakigake	20	3
		Others	48	30
		Total	511	252
		Last election:	July 1993	July 1995

FOREIGN TRADE AND PAYMENTS
(1994, million US dollars)

			Exports	Imports
Commodity exports (fob)	384 176	Percentage distribution:		
Commodity imports (fob)	238 232	OECD countries	51.7	48.2
Services and transfers	−16 804	*of which:* North America	31.5	26.2
Current balance	129 140	South East Asia	35.0	24.7
Long-term capital	−82 037	Other	13.3	27.1
Exports of goods and services in per cent of GDP	9.5	Total	100.0	100.0
Imports of goods and services in per cent of GDP	7.3	Crude material and fuels (SITC 2, 3, 4)	1.2	27.7
		Semi-manufactured goods (5, 6)	16.8	19.2
		Machinery and transport equipment (7)	71.5	19.9
		Other (0, 1, 8, 9)	10.5	33.2
		Total	100.0	100.0

THE CURRENCY

Monetary unit: Yen	Currency units per US$ average of daily figures:	
	Year 1994	102.18
	September 1995	94.59

1. Areas whose population density exceeds 5 000 persons per sq. km.
Note: An international comparison of certain basic statistics is given in an annex table.

This Survey is based on the Secretariat's study prepared for the annual review of Japan by the Economic and Development Review Committee on 18 September 1995.

•

After revisions in the light of discussions during the review, final approval of the Survey for publication was given by the Committee on 9 November 1995.

•

The previous Survey of Japan was issued in November 1994.

Introduction

Japan experienced its third consecutive year of negligible growth in 1994 as the recovery which had appeared promising early in the year proved to be weak. Real GDP increased only $1/2$ per cent before declining in the first half of 1995, while prices have been falling since mid-1994. One factor responsible for the aborted recovery was the sharp appreciation of the yen in early 1995, which adversely affected consumer and business confidence. However, it also reflected the persistent weakness of asset prices, which has, in turn, exacerbated the balance-sheet problems in the banking sector.

Macroeconomic policies have been used extensively by the government in an effort to spark a recovery. Monetary conditions were substantially eased in the first half of 1994 and again during 1995, when the Bank of Japan gradually pushed short-term interest rates down to $1/2$ per cent. Income tax cuts, rising public works expenditure and increased government loans for housing also supported domestic demand in 1994. However, with the effects of these fiscal stimuli beginning to fade, the government in September 1995 introduced a new economic package including increased government investment. Consequently, the budget deficit remained large, thereby increasing Japan's already high level of public debt. In addition to this expansionary policy stance, the government has continued to emphasise deregulation to boost potential output growth.

The stimulatory policy measures put in place in 1995, together with the fall in the value of the yen, should ensure that economic growth revives to around 2 per cent in 1996 with the likelihood that the recovery may accelerate in the course of the year. The upturn should be led by a continued rise in business investment, reflecting improved corporate profitability and better prospects for exports. Consumption spending by households should also pick up, although it may be limited by employment prospects and falling asset prices. Any renewed

1

appreciation of the yen could worsen business sentiment and pose a risk to the pace of the recovery.

Chapter I examines the reasons for the faltering recovery and discusses the short-term outlook. Chapter II assesses the stance of macroeconomic policies as well as the government's approach to resolving the financial sector's problems. Recent progress in deregulation is reviewed in Chapter III. One aspect of structural reform – liberalisation of the distribution system – is analysed in detail in Chapter IV. Conclusions are presented in Chapter V.

Table 1. **Demand and output**

Percentage change from previous period at 1985 prices

| | 1991 | 1992 | 1993 | 1994 | Seasonally-adjusted annual rates | | 1995 |
| | | | | | 1994 | | |
					1st half	2nd half	1st half
Consumption	**2.1**	**1.8**	**1.1**	**2.3**	**2.9**	**1.5**	**0.7**
Private	2.2	1.7	1.0	2.2	3.0	1.3	0.4
Public	1.6	2.7	1.7	2.8	2.1	3.0	3.2
Gross fixed investment	**3.7**	**–1.1**	**–1.8**	**–2.4**	**–4.6**	**0.9**	**–0.9**
Public	4.7	15.3	16.5	5.0	5.1	1.9	–5.1
Private residential	–8.2	–6.7	2.5	9.7	5.7	7.4	–8.0
Private non-residential	6.6	–4.7	–9.3	–8.9	–11.8	–1.6	3.7
Stockbuilding[1]	**0.3**	**–0.5**	**–0.2**	**0.2**	**0.5**	**0.2**	**0.1**
Total domestic demand	**2.9**	**0.3**	**–0.0**	**0.9**	**1.0**	**1.4**	**0.3**
Exports of goods and services	**5.2**	**5.2**	**1.3**	**5.1**	**8.8**	**6.9**	**6.7**
Total demand	**3.2**	**0.9**	**0.1**	**1.5**	**1.9**	**2.2**	**1.2**
Imports of goods and services	**–4.1**	**–0.4**	**2.7**	**8.4**	**9.2**	**11.0**	**11.0**
GDP	**4.3**	**1.1**	**–0.2**	**0.5**	**1.0**	**0.9**	**–0.3**
Memorandum:							
Net exports[1]	1.3	0.8	–0.2	–0.4	0.0	–0.6	–0.6
Industrial production	1.7	–6.1	–4.5	0.9	1.5	6.3	4.7
Business investment/GDP[2]	19.8	18.2	16.0	14.1	14.3	14.0	14.1
Current external surplus/GDP[2]	2.1	3.2	3.1	2.8	3.0	2.6	2.3

1. Contribution to GDP growth.
2. At current prices, per cent.
Source: EPA and OECD estimates.

of 3.2 per cent in June. Slack economic conditions, combined with structural changes in the retail trade sector, also led to falling prices from the second half of 1994.

The paragraphs below review major economic developments since the beginning of 1994, with particular emphasis on the improvement in the corporate financial situation and the impact of the exchange rate appreciation. This is followed by a discussion of the short-term outlook.

Figure 2. **CONTRIBUTIONS TO GROWTH**[1]

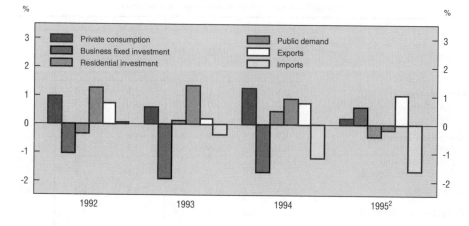

1. The contribution of a demand component to growth equals the change in that component relative to the preceding level of GDP.
2. Figures are for the first semester of 1995 and represent the contribution to growth from the second semester of 1994.
Source: OECD.

Figure 3. **POTENTIAL OUTPUT GROWTH**
Three-year moving average

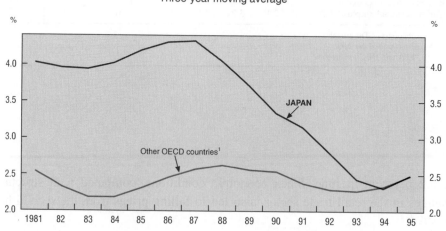

1. Average of 19 OECD countries for which estimates of potential output are available, excluding Japan.
Source: OECD.

6

Improved corporate profitability and investment

Despite generally depressed business conditions, corporate profits, which had deteriorated sharply during the period 1991 to 1993, have been increasing since the beginning of 1994 (Figure 4). Gross operating profits (operating profits plus depreciation) were 8 per cent higher (year-on-year) in the last quarter of 1994 and, relative to sales, are now slightly above their average level in the period 1983 to 1987. The improvement in corporate profitability was strongest in the manufacturing sector, where it was boosted by falling unit costs as production and capacity utilisation increased.[1] Firms' cost-cutting efforts taken in response to the recession and the strong yen (see 1994 Survey) also aided the turnaround in their profitability. In particular, labour costs have been limited by reductions in overtime hours and only slight increases in employment and wages (see below). Moreover, profits were boosted by the decline in interest rates, which lowered the corporate sector's net interest payments by 7 per cent between the fourth quarters of 1993 and 1994.[2]

The increase in corporate profits, coupled with the decline in investment outlays, resulted in a financial surplus for the business sector in 1994 for the first time since 1986 (Figure 4, Panel B). The Ministry of Finance survey of corporate enterprises reports that this surplus was used to pay down debt, which fell relative to sales (Panel C). The sharpest decline was recorded in the short-term debt of real estate companies, which had borrowed heavily during the late 1980s. For all industries excluding real estate, debt decreased 5 per cent relative to sales between the fourth quarters of 1993 and 1994. The decline was largest for loans, reflecting the reduced reliance of firms on banks for financing their activities.

This improvement in the corporate financial situation helped stop the fall in business investment, which had declined from a peak of 20 per cent of GDP in 1991 to 14 per cent in 1994 (Figure 5).[3] Nevertheless, the recovery of investment that began in the second half of 1994 was weak compared with previous cycles. The sluggish increase in private machinery orders, a leading indicator of capital investment, suggests that investment growth, which started to gather pace in the first half of 1995, may have slowed down again in the second half. The pickup of investment has been limited by low capacity utilisation, which remains near the trough levels recorded during the two previous recessions. Indeed, in the manufacturing sector, the number of firms that increased investment to expand capac-

Figure 4. **INDICATORS OF COMPANIES' FINANCIAL POSITION**

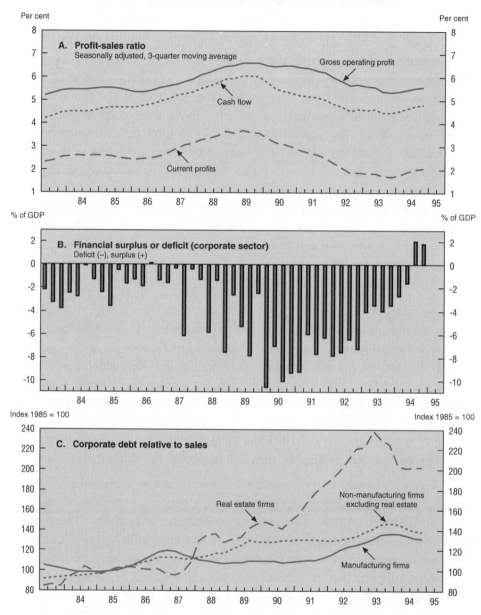

Source : Ministry of Finance, *Financial Statements of Incorporated Businesses*; Bank of Japan, *Flow of Funds Accounts*; EPA, *Annual Report on National Accounts.*

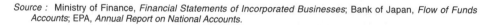

8

Figure 5. **BUSINESS INVESTMENT AND CAPITAL STOCK**

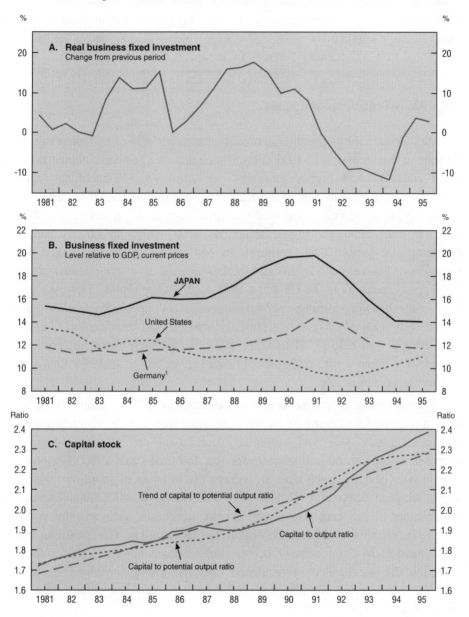

1. West Germany before 1991.
Source: OECD.

9

ity declined for the fourth consecutive year. Investment was also limited by the trend towards greater overseas production by Japanese firms in order to remain internationally competitive despite the strong yen. Consequently, the share of investment that was located overseas increased in FY 1994.[4]

Sluggish private consumption

Real household disposable income increased in 1994 at its fastest rate since the start of the recession in 1991 (Figure 6), reflecting personal income tax cuts, lower inflation and higher earnings per employee. Households received Y 5.5 trillion in 1994 as part of the temporary income tax reduction. The pickup in earnings resulted from increased overtime compensation (Table 2), the first such rise since 1990, and higher bonus payments, which are closely correlated with corporate profits. Basic earnings, though, continued to be affected by the weakness of business conditions and the labour market, which resulted in record low wage agreements in the 1994 and 1995 spring wage rounds. Despite sluggish basic wage growth, earnings per employee picked up in 1994, although the impact on household income was partially offset by the deceleration of employment growth (see below). Meanwhile, business and investment income, which accounts for about a fifth of household receipts, stabilised in 1994 after a sharp decline the previous year.

The income tax cuts received by households in 1994, combined with low interest rates and the timing of the product replacement cycle, boosted purchases of durable goods. This was particularly true in the case of cars, where sales increased in the second half of 1994 for the first time since 1990. The previous peak in sales of cars, which have an average life in Japan of about five and a half years, occurred between 1988 and 1990.[5] Increased sales of other appliances, such as the 12 per cent rise in refrigerator purchases, reflected the boom in housing investment in 1994. According to the Housing Loan Corporation, households spend about five times as much on durable consumer goods during the year following the purchase of a residence than the average working household. Spending on travel, both domestic and overseas, also rose sharply from the second quarter of 1994.

After increasing strongly at the beginning of 1994, personal consumption has failed to keep pace with the increase in real disposable income and the saving

Figure 6. **PERSONAL SECTOR DEMAND**

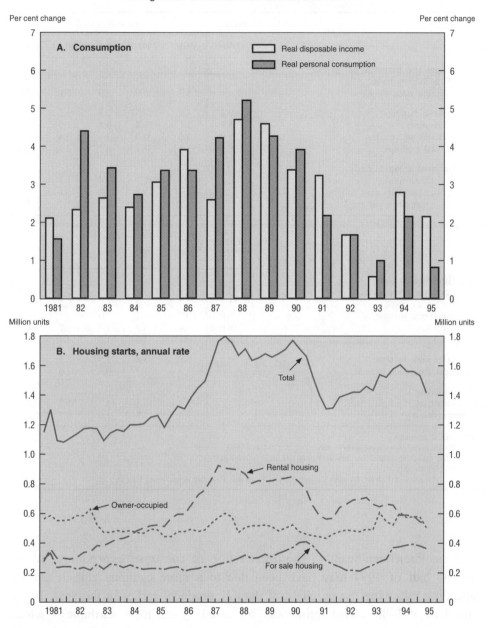

Per cent change

A. Consumption

☐ Real disposable income
▨ Real personal consumption

Million units

B. Housing starts, annual rate

Total

Rental housing

Owner-occupied

For sale housing

Source: EPA and OECD.

11

Table 2.   **Wages, earnings and household income**

	Per cent of total (1994)	Per cent increase				
		1991	1992	1993	1994	1995[1]
A. Wages and earnings, per capita						
Wage survey basis						
Spring wage round	..	5.7	5.0	3.9	3.1	2.8
Basic earnings	69.4	4.0	3.5	2.8	2.7	2.5
Overtime	5.6	−2.1	−10.8	−6.3	1.0	7.8
Bonus payments	25.0	3.6	0.9	−3.1	0.4	1.8
Total earnings	100.0	3.5	1.7	0.7	2.1	2.3
National accounts basis						
Total earnings	..	4.3	2.1	0.4	1.1	0.9
Social security contributions	..	4.0	−3.2	3.0	5.1	3.6
Compensation per employee	..	4.2	1.3	0.7	1.7	1.3

	Per cent of total (1993)	Per cent increase				
		1991	1992	1993	1994[1]	1995[1]
B. Household income						
Employee compensation	63.4	7.8	3.7	2.3	2.4	1.7
Business income[2]	11.1	2.0	4.8	−6.6	−0.2	−0.1
Investment income[3]	6.0	10.9	−7.2	−2.0	..	..
Transfers	19.6	4.4	6.3	3.9	4.2	6.2
Total receipts	100.0	6.7	3.6	1.3	2.3	2.3
Disposable income	..	5.8	3.8	1.9	3.1	1.5
Real disposable income	..	3.3	1.7	0.6	2.8	2.2
Memorandum:						
Saving rate	..	15.1	15.1	14.7	15.2	16.3
Employment growth[4]	..	3.5	2.3	1.6	0.7	0.4

1. OECD estimates.
2. Business and investment income combined in 1994 and 1995.
3. After deducting interest on consumer debt and other interest paid.
4. Employees only.
Source: Ministry of Labour, *Monthly Labour Survey*; Economic Planning Agency and OECD.

rate has risen significantly. The deceleration of consumer expenditures in the second half of 1994 may have been due to a more cautious attitude toward spending following the purchase of durable products earlier in the year. In the first half of 1995, consumption was depressed by the Kobe earthquake, which reduced expenditures in that area, and the appreciation of the yen, which weakened consumer confidence. This reflects the impact of exchange rate changes on

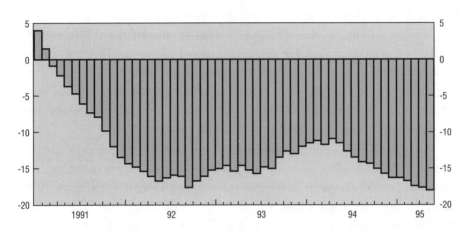

Figure 7. **USED APARTMENT PRICES IN TOKYO**
Year on year percentage increase
Yen per square metre

Source: Recruit Real Estate.

households' expectations of future employment conditions (EPA 1994). There is indeed concern that the yen's strength may force companies to accelerate changes in the lifetime employment practice, for competitiveness considerations, which would result in a significant rise in the unemployment rate.[6] This fear and the erosion of household wealth stemming from the accelerating decline in house prices (Figure 7) seem to have outweighed the positive impact that falling inflation usually has on consumption.[7]

Slowdown of housing investment and public works expenditure

The number of housing starts has declined since the second half of 1994 when it had reached a level only 9 per cent below the 1990 peak (Figure 6, Panel B). Such a fall resulted, in part, from the rise in the Housing Loan Corporation lending rate, which went up from 3.6 to 4.35 per cent during the course of 1994, thus reducing the demand for loans. In addition, the Corporation tightened its credit terms in the fall of 1994 in order to improve the quality of its new loans.[8] Nevertheless, given the large increase in housing loans included in the government fiscal packages implemented between August 1992 and February 1994, this type of credit continued to increase at an annual rate of 15 per cent during the first half of 1995.[9] The continued fall in prices helped, though, to end the boom in condominium construction, which had been boosted by demand from first-time home buyers attracted by falls in interest rates. The end of the special financing provided for rental housing built on agricultural land also depressed housing starts. Moreover, reconstruction efforts in Kobe have not had a large impact on housing starts thus far, reflecting the time needed for city planners to approve new projects and the reluctance of quake victims to assume new debts when their economic future is still uncertain.[10]

Public works expenditure, which had increased at a 15 per cent annual rate between 1991 and 1993, slowed progressively during 1994, recording only a 5 per cent rise for the year, and remained subdued at the beginning of 1995. In contrast to previous fiscal packages, which had increased public works spending by an amount equivalent to 2.2 per cent of GDP over 1992-93, the impact of the February 1994 budget stimulus on public works expenditure was limited. Despite the deceleration, this category of expenditures accounted for almost half of the increase in total domestic demand in 1994. Moreover, its 7 per cent share in GDP remains about double the average in the other OECD countries.

Rising unemployment

The demand for labour continued to fall in 1994 as a result of declining overtime hours and a continued fall in scheduled working hours, in line with the FY 1988 labour law which shortened the standard work week (Figure 8).[11] Despite the continued reduction in hours worked in 1994, employment remained flat (Table 3): increased employment in construction, public utilities and some service industries was offset by the manufacturing sector, which shed jobs at a more rapid pace than in any downturn other than that following the first oil shock. In addition, the number of workers in the distribution sector fell in 1994. Consequently, total employment in the private sector declined slightly but this was offset by continued growth in government employment. The demand for labour in the business sector, though, stabilised at the beginning of 1995 at a level 5 per cent below the peak of the previous cycle reflecting an increase in overtime hours, primarily in the manufacturing sector.

The wholesale price index of goods sold in the domestic market declined by almost 2 per cent in 1994 before stabilising somewhat in the early part of 1995. This index remains below other broad measures of inflation because of the decline in output prices in the Japanese manufacturing sector since 1985, with the exception of the food industry (Figure 10). There have been particularly large falls in the prices of electrical machinery, which includes electronics, and in chemical industries. The differences in price movements generally reflect different rates of increase of productivity, since industries have faced similar changes in their labour and capital costs. Despite the fall in the GDP deflator in the manufacturing sector, the overall GDP deflator was rising until mid-1994 as a result of higher growth of prices in the public sector as well as in construction, real estate and other service industries in the private sector.

In contrast to the GDP deflator and the wholesale prices of goods, the consumer price index (CPI) has not yet shown a deflationary trend. Although there have been declines in some recent months, this is largely due to fluctuations in food prices. Core CPI inflation, which excludes food and energy, has been stable in recent months with a year-on-year increase of 0.1 per cent in July 1995.

Figure 10. **AVERAGE INFLATION RATE BY INDUSTRY**
1985-1993, GDP deflator at producer values

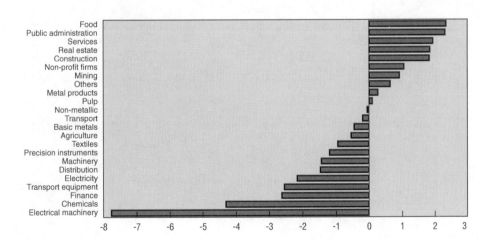

Source: National Accounts.

19

Figure 11. **COMPONENTS OF THE CPI**

Percentage changes over previous year

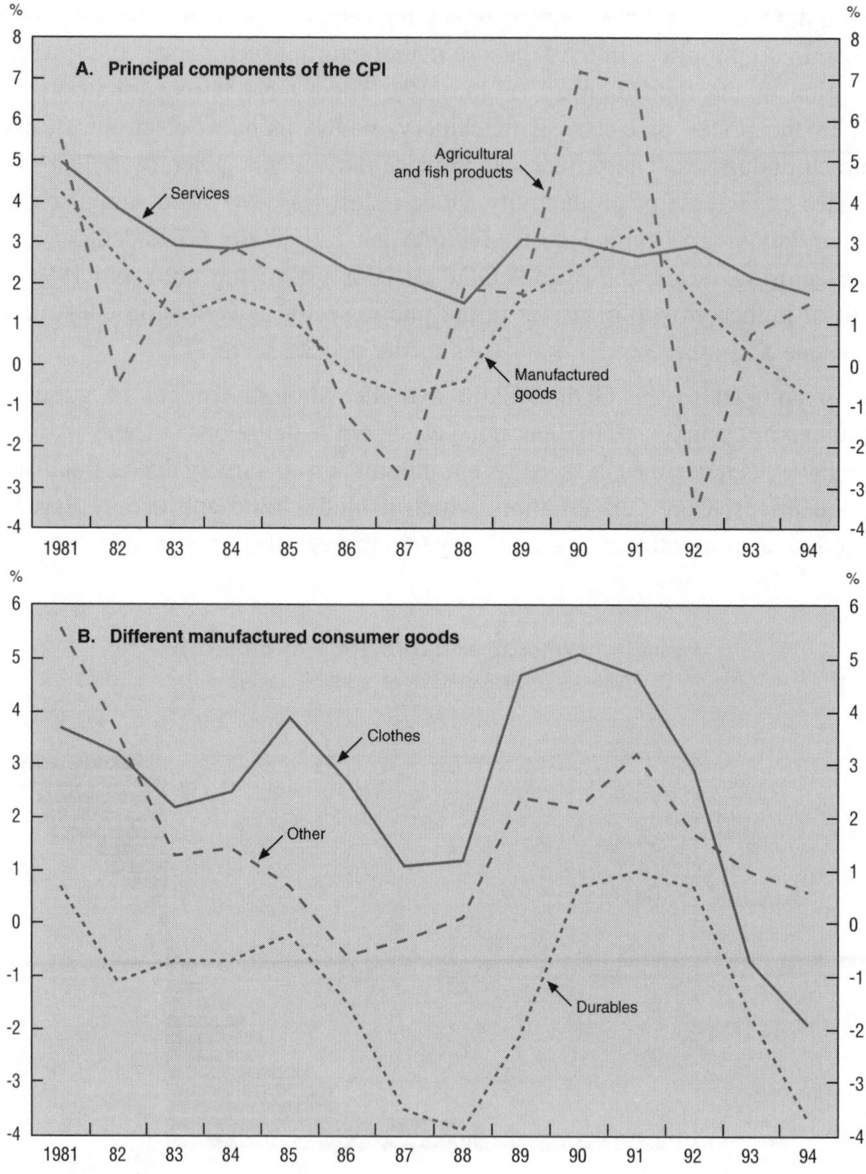

%

A. Principal components of the CPI

Services

Agricultural
and fish products

Manufactured
goods

1981 82 83 84 85 86 87 88 89 90 91 92 93 94

%

B. Different manufactured consumer goods

Clothes

Other

Durables

1981 82 83 84 85 86 87 88 89 90 91 92 93 94

Source: Management and Coordination Agency, *Report on the consumer price index.*

20

The stability of the CPI in the face of falling prices of manufactured goods reflects the high weight given to services and rent (48 per cent) and agricultural and fishery products (10 per cent). The services component of the CPI has continued to increase steadily at between 2 and 3 per cent annually (Figure 11, Panel A). Meanwhile, the goods component of the index – which measures the prices paid by consumers in shops – turned negative in early 1994, reflecting falling output prices in the manufacturing sector and changes in the retail system.[17] The decline in prices was largest for durable goods (Figure 11, Panel B). In addition, the price of clothing, which accounts for 7 per cent of expenditures, started to decline for the first time in 1993. This represents a marked contrast from the late 1980s, when clothing recorded some of the sharpest price increases.

While the large weight of services has delayed declines in the CPI and the personal consumption deflator, other forms of expenditure which are concentrated in goods have experienced falling price levels. The long-term decline in the absolute and relative price of business investment goods has continued (Figure 12) while the price of housing and government investment have also fallen

Figure 12. **THE MOVEMENT OF EXPENDITURE DEFLATORS RELATIVE TO THE GDP DEFLATOR**[1]

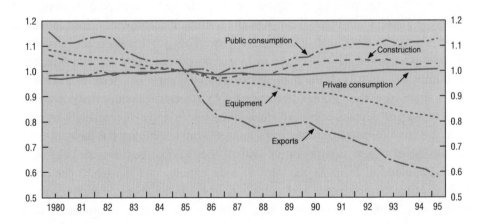

1. A decline in an expenditure deflator relative to the GDP deflator shows that the deflator has been increasing less rapidly than the overall price level.
Source: OECD.

slightly. The steepest decline continues to be in the price of exports of goods and services, which have fallen at a 4 per cent annual rate relative to the GDP deflator since 1980.

Continued external adjustment

Japan has been steadily losing international competitiveness since 1990 (Figure 13). After a pause in 1994, Japan's relative export prices and unit labour costs resumed their upward trend at the beginning of 1995 as the exchange rate appreciated. Japanese firms, though, have been able to significantly moderate the adverse impacts of the yen's rise on their export volumes by reducing their export prices in yen terms to a certain extent. This is evidenced by the fact that the loss in competitiveness, as measured by relative export prices, is smaller than that using either relative unit labour costs or the "real" effective exchange rate.[18] By the first half of 1995, export prices (in yen terms), were 17 per cent lower than in the second half of 1992, indicating that almost half of the appreciation of the effective exchange rate appreciation over that period had been offset by price reductions by Japanese manufacturers.[19]

Despite the decline in Japan's international competitiveness, export volume growth accelerated to 5 per cent in 1994 and accelerated further in the first half of 1995. However, the pick up in exports, which reflected a marked acceleration of demand in Japan's major markets, was not sufficient to prevent a loss in export market share for the fourth consecutive year. The gap between the growth in Japanese exports and the expansion in Japan's export markets reached 6 percentage points, up slightly from 5 points in 1993 (Figure 14). The extent of the market share loss, though, has been limited by structural factors that have made the demand for Japanese exports less sensitive to price increases.[20] Japanese producers have responded to the yen's appreciating trend over the past decade by specialising in capital equipment as part of their global business strategy. Consumer durables fell from 31 per cent of total exports in 1985 to 20 per cent in 1994 as Japanese producers lost competitiveness in audiovisual equipment and white goods. This was offset by a rise in the share of capital equipment exports from 48 to 62 per cent over the same period. Asian countries have accounted for a large share of the increase: in 1994, Japan's capital equipment exports to the Dynamic Asian Economies increased by 20 per cent. As a result, Asia's share of

Figure 13. **INTERNATIONAL COMPETITIVENESS**

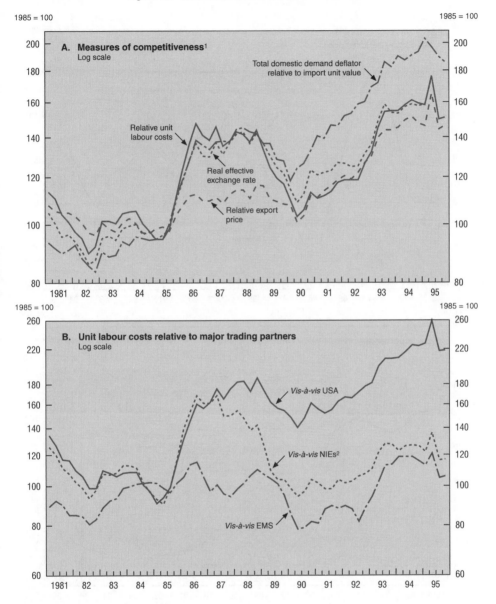

1. Calculated *vis-à-vis* twenty-four countries including the four Asian Nies.
2. Hong Kong, Korea, Taiwan and Singapore.
Source: OECD.

Figure 14. **EXPORT AND IMPORT PERFORMANCE**[1]

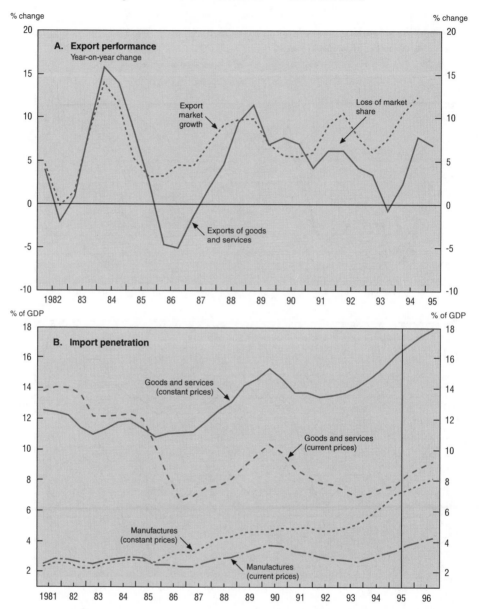

% change

% change

A. Export performance
Year-on-year change

Export market growth

Loss of market share

Exports of goods and services

1982 83 84 85 86 87 88 89 90 91 92 93 94 95

% of GDP

% of GDP

B. Import penetration

Goods and services (constant prices)

Goods and services (current prices)

Manufactures (constant prices)

Manufactures (current prices)

1981 82 83 84 85 86 87 88 89 90 91 92 93 94 95 96

1. The vertical line indicates the end of the historical period and the beginning of the projection period.
Source: OECD.

24

Japanese exports increased from 24 per cent in 1985 to 40 per cent in 1994 while the share of the OECD area declined from 62 to 52 per cent. A significant portion of the increased sales to Asia was due to the growing number of Japanese-owned production facilities in the region that depend on inputs sourced from Japan (see below).

The appreciation of the yen has also contributed to a marked acceleration in import growth. Imports met about two-thirds of the increase in demand in 1994 and even more in the first half of 1995, thereby substantially subtracting from GDP growth. Part of the rise was due to the increasing sensitivity of the demand for imports to prices during the past few years (in contrast to the falling sensitivity of foreign demand for Japanese exports).[21] This phenomenon, which has magnified the volume response to falling import prices, is a result of the growing share of manufactured consumer goods in Japanese imports.[22] Overall, manufactured imports increased 45 per cent in volume terms over the past three years, boosting their share of total imports to almost two-thirds in 1994 compared with less than one-third ten years ago. As a result, import penetration, measured in constant prices, increased significantly, particularly for manufactured goods (Figure 14, Panel B).

Asian countries accounted for much of the increase in Japanese imports. Between 1990 and 1994, the share of China and ASEAN countries (Thailand, Malaysia, Singapore, the Philippines, Indonesia and Brunei) in total manufactured imports has more than doubled (Figure 15), with the increase concentrated in certain industries. For example, China's share of Japanese imports has risen to 60 per cent for clothing and to over 50 per cent for toys. The market share of ASEAN countries has been rising particularly rapidly in audiovisual and domestic electrical equipment. By 1993, their shares of Japanese imports of televisions and video recorders, which were close to zero in 1989, had reached 75 and 50 per cent, respectively, while for washing machines, it had risen to around 70 per cent.

The rapid rise in imports contributed to a 27 per cent decline in the real trade surplus in 1994. In nominal terms, the trade balance, measured in yen, fell at a slower pace, reflecting a decline in import prices that may have been due to a shift towards imports from East Asia. The fall in the trade surplus was accompanied by a decline in the surplus on investment income. As a result, by the first half of 1995, the current-account surplus had fallen by almost 24 per cent in yen terms since the first half of 1994 to reach (as noted) 2.3 per cent of GDP.

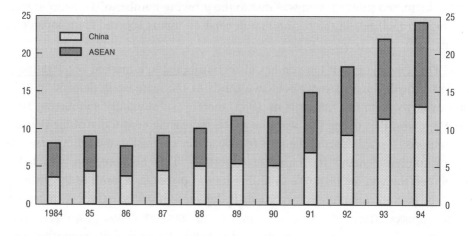

Figure 15. **THE SHARE OF MANUFACTURED IMPORTS FROM CHINA AND ASEAN COUNTRIES**[1]

1. ASEAN refers to Thailand, Singapore, Malaysia, Brunei, Philippines and Indonesia.
Source: Ministry of Finance.

However, with the fall in the value of the dollar, the current-account surplus in dollars has remained broadly constant during this period at around $130 billion (Table 4).

Direct investment abroad accounts for a considerable portion of the capital outflow associated with this current-account surplus. Much of this investment has been located in Asia (Table 5). Between 1990 and 1994, Asia's share of Japan's total overseas investment in manufacturing almost doubled from 20 to 38 per cent. About 16 per cent of the output produced by Japanese subsidiaries in Asia is exported to Japan. In the electrical machinery industry, the proportion of output sold in Japan was 27 per cent, with an additional 8 per cent exported to Europe and North America. The integration of Asian plants in worldwide production and distribution networks reflects the importance of cost-cutting as a motive for investment in this region. Indeed, direct investment in Asia is closely linked to the effective exchange rate.[23] Labour costs are also important; in a 1992 survey of Japanese manufacturing firms investing overseas, a fourth cited lower labour costs as the motivation for investing in ASEAN countries.[24]

Table 4. **External balances**

$ billion

| | 1991 | 1992 | 1993 | 1994 | Seasonally-adjusted annual rates | | |
| | | | | | 1994 | | 1995 |
					1st half	2nd half	1st quarter
Trade	**103.0**	**132.3**	**141.5**	**145.9**	**146.7**	**143.7**	**147.2**
Exports	306.6	330.9	351.3	384.2	371.8	395.3	437.3
Imports	203.5	198.5	209.8	238.2	225.1	251.5	290.1
Services	**−17.7**	**−10.1**	**−3.9**	**−9.3**	**0.3**	**−18.9**	**−11.4**
Transportation[1]	−10.3	−10.0	−11.2	−12.6	−10.9	−14.3	−15.3
Travel[1]	−20.5	−23.2	−23.3	−27.2	−25.2	−29.2	−30.9
Investment income[1]	26.7	36.2	41.4	41.0	46.5	35.5	46.9
Other services[1]	−13.6	−13.1	−10.9	−10.5	−10.0	−10.9	−12.1
Transfers	**−12.5**	**−4.7**	**−6.1**	**−7.5**	**−6.8**	**−8.2**	**−8.9**
Private transfer[1]	−0.6	−1.3	−2.2	−2.8	−2.4	−3.2	−3.7
Official transfer[1]	−11.8	−3.4	−3.9	−4.7	−4.4	−5.0	−5.3
Current account	**72.9**	**117.6**	**131.5**	**129.1**	**134.4**	**123.7**	**119.9**
Memorandum:							
Volume growth, per cent[2]							
Exports	2.5	1.5	−1.7	1.7	3.7	5.7	5.4
Imports	4.0	−0.4	4.2	13.4	15.0	17.7	12.5
of which: Manufactures	6.3	−2.2	8.3	18.3	22.4	23.6	27.0
Unit value dollars, per cent[2]							
Exports	6.9	6.4	8.1	7.8	8.2	6.4	16.0
Imports	−3.0	−1.2	−0.8	0.6	−2.4	8.8	12.4
Current balance (trillion yen)	9.8	14.9	14.6	13.2	14.2	12.2	10.8
(per cent of GDP)	2.2	3.2	3.0	2.6	3.0	2.6	2.3

1. Not seasonally adjusted.
2. Custom clearance basis (service trade is not included), year-on-year.
Source: Bank of Japan, *Balance of Payments Monthly*, OECD.

In contrast, output by Japanese plants in Europe and the United States is primarily sold in the local market, with less than 3 per cent exported to Japan.[25] Consequently, investment in these regions has followed movements in local demand, with the exchange rate playing a relatively insignificant role – at least until 1993. Japanese investment in Europe and the United States, though, has been unprofitable with manufacturing industries losing money in 1992, although Japan's US subsidiaries moved into profit in 1993 (Table 6). This poor performance may reflect the fact that some of the investment in Europe and the

Table 5. Japanese direct investment abroad

$ billion, fiscal years

	1990	1991	1992	1993	1994
Total	56.9	41.6	34.1	36.0	41.1
Manufacturing	15.5	12.3	10.1	11.1	13.8
By industry					
Electrical machinery	5.7	2.3	1.8	2.8	2.6
Transport machinery	1.9	2.0	1.0	0.9	2.0
Chemicals	2.3	1.6	2.0	1.7	2.6
Metals	1.0	0.9	0.8	0.8	1.0
Other	4.6	5.5	4.2	4.9	5.6
By area					
Asia	3.1	2.9	3.1	3.7	5.2
Other	12.4	9.4	7.0	7.4	8.6
Non-manufacturing	40.6	28.8	23.7	24.6	26.9
By industry					
Finance and real estate	19.2	13.9	9.7	12.5	9.5
Services and commerce	17.5	10.7	10.2	8.6	11.5
Other	3.9	4.2	3.8	3.5	5.9
By area					
Asia	4.0	3.0	3.3	3.0	4.2
Other	36.6	25.8	20.4	21.6	22.7

Source: Ministry of Finance.

United States was aimed at establishing manufacturing bases behind trade barriers and to avoid trade friction.[26] In contrast, Japanese manufacturing investment in Asia recorded an average profit-to-sales ratio that was almost triple that

Table 6. Profitability of Japanese overseas manufacturing operations

Current after-tax profit as per cent of sales

	Asia		Europe		United States		Domestic companies	
	1992	1993	1992	1993	1992	1993	1992	1993
Textiles	7.3	5.3	0.1	−0.9	3.0	0.6	1.9	..
Chemicals	4.8	4.0	−2.6	−2.0	−1.0	0.2	2.3	..
General machinery	3.2	4.7	−3.4	−4.2	1.0	−1.6	1.0	..
Electrical machinery	2.4	3.4	−2.3	−0.6	0.0	0.5	0.7	..
Transportation machinery	4.4	5.0	−4.8	−1.8	0.5	2.2	1.1	..
All manufacturing	3.3	3.8	−2.8	−1.0	−1.0	0.1	1.3	..

Source: MITI, *Basic survey of business activities abroad.*

28

achieved in Japan. Subsidiaries in the labour-intensive textile industry were particularly profitable as a result of lower labour costs in Asia.

With the increase in foreign direct investment, Japanese overseas production increased at a 6½ per cent annual rate between 1989 and 1994, while domestic production fell. As a result, the share of manufacturing output produced overseas has risen to over 8 per cent and almost one in ten employees of Japanese manufacturing corporations is now located abroad (Table 7). In certain industries, notably transport machinery, the share of overseas production is markedly higher, reflecting the need to avoid trade barriers. The share is also high for the electrical equipment industry, which faces especially strong pressure to lower costs. The overall share of overseas production, though, is still low compared with the United States and Germany, where it was as high as 26 and 16 respectively in 1992.[27] Many smaller Japanese companies have no overseas plants. For Japanese companies with at least one plant abroad, the proportion of overseas output rises to almost 21 per cent. Business surveys suggest that both the scale of multina-

Table 7. **Japanese manufacturing production overseas**

Percentage of domestic production

	1989	1990	1991	1992	1993	1994
Foodstuffs	1.3	1.2	1.2	1.3	2.4	..
Textiles	1.3	3.1	2.6	2.3	3.2	..
Paper	1.9	2.1	1.6	1.4	1.9	..
Chemicals	3.8	5.1	5.5	4.8	7.0	..
Metals	5.3	5.6	4.9	5.0	6.3	..
Ceramics	6.4	5.2	5.2	7.8	6.5	..
General machinery	3.8	10.6	7.6	4.1	5.8	..
Electrical machinery	11.0	11.4	11.0	10.8	12.6	..
Transport machinery	14.3	12.6	13.7	17.5	17.3	..
Precision machinery	5.4	4.7	4.4	3.6	5.6	..
Petroleum refining	0.1	0.2	1.2	5.2	7.1	..
Other	3.1	3.1	2.6	2.3	2.8	..
All manufacturing	5.7	6.4	6.0	6.2	7.4	8.2
Multinational manufacturers	..	..	16.7	17.3	18.3	20.9
Memorandum item:						
Employment in overseas plants						
Millions	1.1	0.9	1.2	1.3	1.1	1.5
Per cent of domestic employment	7.4	6.0	7.7	8.3	7.2	10.8

Source: MITI, *Basic survey of business activities abroad.*

29

tional operations and the number of companies investing abroad for the first time will increase markedly in the next three years.

Short-term outlook: a sustainable recovery?

Activity seems to be remaining weak in the second half of 1995. Corporate surveys conducted during the summer suggested that businessmen's evaluation of the economic situation had deteriorated and that industrial output would be no higher at the end of the year than at the beginning (Figure 16). As a result, companies seem likely to reduce stocks, and the growth of business investment may pause temporarily in the second half of the year. Also, consumption still appears to be sluggish and, given the fall in housing starts in the first half of the year, investment in this area seems likely to decline. In contrast, public investment should increase in line with the policy of front-loading expenditure at the beginning of the current fiscal year. The fall of the yen in the late summer is unlikely to influence exports much before the end of the year, so that output

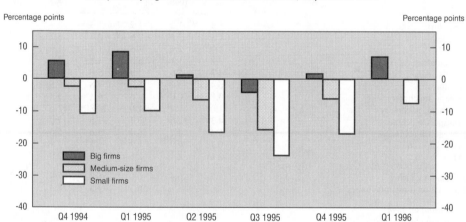

Figure 16. **CHANGE IN THE BUSINESS CLIMATE**
Companies judgement on business conditions, September 1995[1]

1. The judgement about business conditions reflects the difference between those companies expecting an upturn in the economy and those expecting a downturn.
Source: Ministry of Finance, Business Survey.

growth in the second half of 1995 is estimated at just ³/₄ per cent, bringing the increase in overall activity for the year to only ¹/₄ per cent.

Economic activity is projected to progressively pick up during 1996, raising growth to just under 2 per cent on average (Table 8). The major assumptions underlying the projections are the following:

- the exchange rate will stabilise at Y 103 to the dollar;
- short-term interest rates will remain stable from the second half of 1995 through 1996 at about ¹/₂ per cent while long-term rates will rise by ¹/₂ percentage point to about 3¹/₂ per cent by the end of 1996;
- oil prices will rise 8 per cent in 1995 to $16.7 per barrel and remain constant in real terms thereafter;
- Japan's export market for manufactures will grow about 11 per cent in 1995 and 9 per cent in 1996.

The reduction in the discount rate and short-term money market rates, the September economic package and the fall in the value of the currency may ensure that the growth of domestic demand picks up during 1996. Private non-residential investment is expected to be particularly buoyant, given the favourable outlook for profits in the current low interest rate environment. Firms in the leading sectors of the economy, such as electronics, are planning large increases as are industries such as pulp and paper. In other areas, such as metals, shipbuilding and car manufacturing, the improved profitability stemming from the fall in the yen may add to plans for rationalisation investment.

As the economy starts to grow more firmly, consumers are expected to regain confidence and overcome current concerns about employment prospects, although labour-intensive sectors of the manufacturing industry will still be under pressure. As a result, the household savings ratio should stabilise and the growth of consumption may accelerate. Housing investment is projected to grow slightly but only because of the substantial rebuilding effort that may get under way in the Kobe area, where, to cope with the consequences of the earthquake, the regional government has promised to construct 125 000 houses over the next three years. Finance for public works in this area has been provided in the latest economic package. More generally, this package should ensure that public investment starts to grow once again in 1996, in line with the ten-year public investment programme.

Table 8. **Short-term prospects**

Percentage change from previous year

	1994 Current prices (¥ trillion)	1993	1994	1995	1996
Demand and output (volume)					
Private consumption	277.7	1.0	2.2	0.8	1.8
Government consumption	46.1	1.7	2.8	2.6	2.2
Gross fixed investment	134.1	−1.8	−2.4	0.6	3.6
Public [1]	42.0	16.5	5.0	−0.1	6.6
Private residential	25.9	2.5	9.7	−3.9	−0.9
Private non-residential	66.2	−9.3	−8.9	2.2	3.3
Final domestic demand	457.8	0.1	0.8	0.9	2.4
Stockbuilding [2]	1.3	−0.2	0.2	0.0	0.0
Total domestic demand	**459.1**	**0.0**	**0.9**	**0.9**	**2.3**
Exports of goods and services	44.4	1.3	5.0	6.1	5.8
Total demand	**503.6**	**0.1**	**1.5**	**1.6**	**2.8**
Imports of goods and services	34.4	2.7	8.4	10.3	9.1
GDP	**469.1**	**−0.2**	**0.5**	**0.3**	**1.8**
Inflation					
GDP deflator		0.8	0.2	−0.9	−0.4
Private consumption deflator		1.3	0.3	−0.6	−0.3
Production					
Industrial production		−4.5	0.8	2.9	−0.6
Labour market					
Total employment		0.2	0.0	0.1	0.1
Unemployment rate		2.5	2.9	3.2	3.4
Balance of payments ($ billion)					
Exports		351.3	384.2	428.3	431.4
Imports		209.8	238.2	290.4	307.0
Current balance		131.4	129.1	112.3	96.1
(per cent of GDP)		(3.1)	(2.8)	(2.3)	(2.1)
Net exports [2]	10.0	−0.2	−0.4	−0.6	−0.6
General government					
Net lending (per cent of GDP)		−1.4	−3.5	−4.0	−4.7

1. Including public corporations.
2. Contributions to GDP growth.
Source: OECD.

External adjustment is expect to continue in 1996. Companies will likely face further losses in export market shares though at a diminishing rate while imports may supply almost half of the total increase in demand in 1996 as the economy becomes more open. This should reduce the current-account surplus, projected at just over 2 per cent of GDP, thus keeping output growth below that of potential. As a result, capacity utilisation and unemployment may continue to rise. Consequently, the underlying downward pressure on prices could continue, though for consumer prices this may be masked by the pass through of higher import prices.

There is a risk that the above projections may prove to be optimistic. Indeed, even as world demand appears to be weakening, Japanese consumers are increasing their saving in the face of falling asset prices. Moreover, although overall business outlays are rising, some major industries are still cutting their investment plans. In these circumstances, a further negative shock to confidence coming perhaps from a renewed appreciation of the exchange rate might spark further cost cutting and rationalisation in the manufacturing sector, with adverse effects on employment and, in turn, private consumption. This could also accelerate the transfer of production elsewhere in Asia, so adding to the flow of imports. Such a development would aggravate the deflationary pressures which, given the persistent fragility of the financial system, could push the economy back into recession. On the other hand, a further orderly reversal of previous appreciations of the yen would have beneficial effects on corporate and consumer sentiment. With faster growth of consumption and investment, combined with a more modest rise in imports, output growth in 1996 would in this case be higher than currently projected.

Looking beyond 1996, Japan's economy is unlikely to achieve the relatively high growth rate recorded in the second half of the 1980s. One reason is the decline in the working-age population beginning in 1995 and the continued fall in working hours, which will dampen labour inputs though there may be some offsetting increase in participation rates. There is also concern that the increasing share of elderly and part-time workers may diminish the quality of the labour force and its adaptability to new technology. Another factor that may limit growth is an increase in the share of offshore investment by Japanese firms. To remain competitive, Japanese manufacturers are likely to continue to boost production overseas, particularly in Asia. However, as discussed below, these constraints on potential growth could be offset by further deregulation as this would boost productivity, especially in the service sector.

II. Macroeconomic policies

Since 1992 there has been a marked attempt to stimulate domestic demand through both fiscal and monetary policies. After a short interruption in the second half of 1994 when the economy showed signs of recovery, the thrust of policies became once again expansionary from the first half of 1995 onwards, against a background of mounting evidence that economic activity was weakening and that downward pressure on prices was continuing. Indeed, official lending rates were reduced twice and a new economic package was introduced. At the same time, in view of the slow progress in banks' balance sheet adjustment and following the collapse of five financial institutions, the government announced that it was examining the possibility of dealing with difficulties of the financial system by using public money. Such a move would likely increase the need for fiscal consolidation in the medium term. Indeed, together with an unexpected revenue shortfall due to the weakness of the economy, the long-lasting fiscal stimulus has significantly widened the general government deficit to a level comparable to the OECD average. Moreover, gross public debt has been moving towards the high levels seen elsewhere in the OECD area. These developments considerably reduce the fiscal room for manoeuvre.

Monetary management

With the exchange rate rising

The yen's exchange rate has fluctuated markedly during 1995. It rose rapidly at the beginning of the year, reaching a peak of slightly above 80 against the US dollar in April, corresponding to an appreciation of 18 per cent from the average for 1994 (Figure 17, Panel A). This rise was subsequently reversed and, by October, the yen's effective exchange rate had returned to a level slightly below its average of 1994. These developments have taken place despite the discount rate (ODR) to ½ per cent brought the overall decline in short-term interest rates to 180 basis points since the beginning of the year (Figure 19, Panel A). By October 1995, short-term real interest rates were at their lowest since the 1970s (Figure 20). However, real short-term lending rates for new loans have not fallen as much and remain higher than at the trough of the last cycle. In the context of falling bond yields in other OECD countries, long-term rates have

Figure 20. **REAL INTEREST RATES**[1]

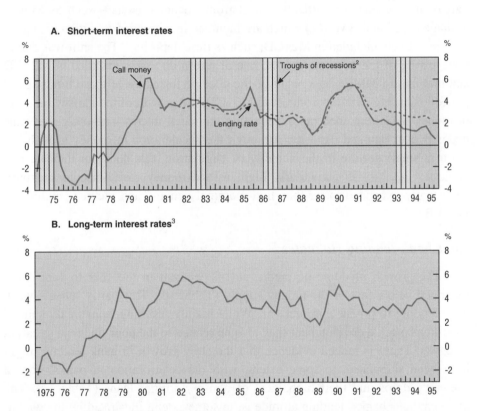

A. **Short-term interest rates**

B. **Long-term interest rates**[3]

1. Measured by the difference between nominal interest rates and the 3-month moving average of the annual inflation rate measured by the consumer price index excluding food and energy.
2. The dating of the phases of the business cycle are those defined by the EPA.
3. Ten-year central government bonds.
Source: OECD.

39

declined by 170 basis points since the beginning of 1995, perhaps reflecting reduced inflation expectations in Japan (Figure 19, Panels A and B). As a result, the yield curve – the spread between short and long-term rates – steepened (Figure 19, Panel C).

...and money growth picked up

The pickup in the growth of the most closely monitored money aggregate (M2+CD), which began in early 1993, accelerated in the second half of 1994 and by the first half of 1995 it was 3¼ per cent higher than a year earlier (Figure 21). Part of this acceleration reflects a shift from financial assets – such as Money Management Funds (MMFs) which are included in a broader definition of liquidity – into assets included in M2+CD, such as time deposits.[30] The shift was due to a narrowing of the gap between the rate of return on assets included in M2+CD and that on the MMFs, as a result of the poor performance of these funds' bond portfolios during 1994. In contrast to M3+CD, the growth of the narrow measure of money (M1) remained rapid, reflecting the small interest-rate margin of time deposits over demand deposits. Although the acceleration in money growth has led to a small decline in the velocity of circulation, this does not indicate that domestic liquidity is particularly high, as the money stock has, in the past, persistently expanded faster than both nominal demand and income (Figure 21, Panel B).

...but bank lending stagnates

The growth of domestic credit, at 1.5 per cent in the year to June 1995 remained below that of the money supply (Table 10). This partly reflects weak bank lending to private corporations. While mainly resulting from weak demand conditions, such a development may also be related to the poor financial situation of banks. There is indeed evidence that the slow growth in bank lending might have been associated, to some extent, with the deterioration in banks' capital adequacy ratios and their high level of non-performing loans (Table 11). The more cautious banks' lending attitude is, to some extent, illustrated by the widening of their interest rate margins on new loans over the past three years (Figure 19).

Lending to the private sector from a broader category of financial institutions progressed more rapidly (by 2.6 per cent during 1994), suggesting a continued shift of demand away from bank lending towards credit granted by public establishments (Figure 22). Rather than reducing interest rate margins on loans to companies, banks increased their purchases of corporate and government bonds, which, in the latter case, have replaced other forms of credit to the public sector. Private companies used the proceeds of domestic bond issues to repay foreign bonds as well as foreign and domestic bank borrowing. Thus, the weakness of overall lending has not been critical for major companies given their comfortable financial position. For smaller companies, on the other hand, the weakness in bank lending may have been a factor restraining their investment.

In sum, the above analysis shows that the monetary stance has become easier since early 1995. Indeed, short-term interest rates are currently at their lowest level and, while bank lending rates have not fallen by the same proportion, the yield curve appears to be the steepest since the late 1970s. Moreover, the reversal of the spring 1995 appreciation of the exchange rate reinforces the impression that, overall, monetary conditions are stimulatory.

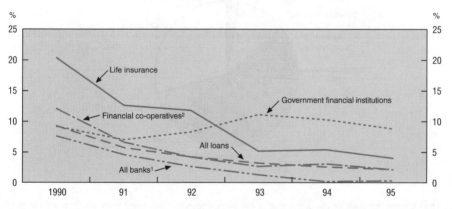

Figure 22. **OUTSTANDING LOANS BY FINANCIAL INSTITUTIONS**
Percentage growth over previous year

1. All banks include city banks, long-term credit banks, trust banks, regional banks, secondary regional banks.
2. Financial co-operatives include Shinkin banks, credit co-operatives, labour credit co-operatives, Shokochukin, Norinchukin, agricultural co-operatives.
Source: Bank of Japan, *Economic Statistic Annual.*

Fragility of the financial system

The difficulties experienced by the Japanese financial sector since the bursting of the speculative bubble are proving to be more serious than thought previously. According to the Ministry of Finance, as much as Y 40 trillion (almost $400 billion) of loans by financial institutions may have been non-performing or subject to restructuring in March 1995, an amount equivalent to 5.8 per cent of their outstanding loans or 8½ per cent of GDP. While the major banks[31] have made progress in reducing their bad loans, more serious problems remain in other parts of the financial system (Figure 23). The following paragraphs provide an assessment of the extent of these problems and of their policy implications.

Figure 23. **THE RELATIVE SIZE OF PRIVATE CREDIT INSTITUTIONS**[1]
March 1995

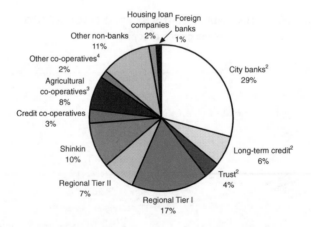

1. The denominator used for the calculation of the percentages includes loans from one institution to another institution.
2. Major banks include city banks, long-term credit banks and trust banks.
3. In addition includes "Norinchukin" banks, credit federations of agricultural co-operatives, fishery co-operatives and credit federation of fishery co-operatives.
4. Other co-operatives include "Shokochukin" banks, labor credit co-operatives.
Source: Ministry of Finance.

Major banks are slowly reducing their bad loans

In March 1995, the major banks (accounting for 39 per cent of total loans by private credit institutions)[32] reported that Y 12.5 trillion or 3.3 per cent of their outstanding loans were non-performing.[33] The government announced that another Y 10 trillion of loans have been restructured with interest payments either reduced or cancelled. In total, these two categories amount to 5.9 per cent of the major banks' loans. By March 1996, banks will have to disclose the amount of these restructured loans. The major banks succeeded in reducing their officially-declared non-performing loans from a peak of Y 13.8 trillion in September 1993 by writing off bad loans or by selling them to the "Co-operative Credit Purchasing Company" (CCPC) – an institution established in January 1993 with the objective of purchasing problem loans from banks at a discount, thereby allowing banks to obtain tax relief on these loans. Equally important, they increased their loss provisions to 34 per cent of remaining non-performing loans by the end of FY 1994.

Overall, while these efforts have significantly reduced the exposure of banks to bad loans (Figure 24), they have led them to declare losses in FY 1994. Indeed, total bad loan charges (the sum of write-offs, losses on sales to the CCPC and loss provisions) exceeded net operating profits by 40 per cent in FY 1994. In order to minimise their accounting losses, major banks revalued some of their equity portfolio at a profit, which, combined with the decline in the stock market, had the effect of reducing banks' unrealised capital gains by over half in the year to March 1995.[34] This, in turn, lowered their average risk-adjusted capital-adequacy ratio to 8.9 per cent in March 1995 from 9.7 per cent a year earlier.

The banks' capital ratios are particularly sensitive to movements in the stock market as unrealised gains are estimated to change by about Y 1 trillion for each 1 per cent movement in share prices. Banks' capital position is also linked to the movement of the yen as about 30 per cent of city banks' assets and liabilities are denominated in foreign currencies. As a result, an appreciation of the yen tends to strengthen banks' balance sheets. Thus, to the extent that falls in the stock market are associated with rises in the exchange rate, the banks' exposure to these two factors taken together remains unaffected. Moreover, the major banks' overall capital is now much less dependent on unrealised gains than in the past, as they have issued significant amounts of subordinated debt, preferred stock and even

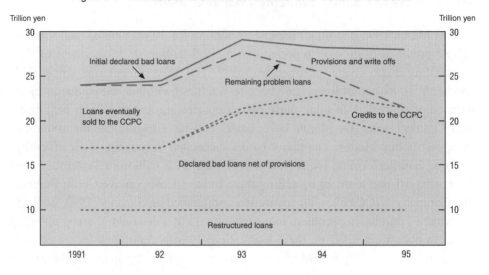

Figure 24. **THE DECLINE IN MAJOR BANKS' BAD LOAN EXPOSURE**

Source: Federation of Japanese Banks, Ministry of Finance and OECD estimates.

perpetual debt. Nevertheless, although comparisons are difficult since accounting conventions differ across countries, the core capital of Japanese banks was, in 1993, relatively low by international standards[35] (Figure 25).

Healthy operating profits are an important precondition for further balance-sheet consolidation and increased loan loss provisions. Given their current level of profits, the major banks could completely write off non-performing loans in three years, without further reducing their capital base (Table 12). Full provisioning, however, may not be required since the problem loans may have some residual value once collateral has been sold. For instance, if the residual value of the loans was the same as for those sold recently to the CCPC,[36] the major banks would need a further Y 4 trillion of provisions to fully cover their exposure to bad loans, representing about eighteen months' operating profit. Nonetheless, providing loss provisions for restructured loans may require the banks to revalue more of their equity portfolios.[37] Banks may also be able to revalue their real estate holdings currently in their balance sheets at historic cost. However, the aggregate position conceals the problems of a few banks which have extremely

46

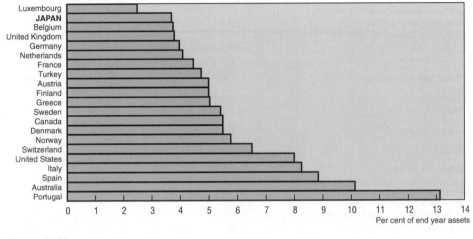

Figure 25. **BANK CAPITAL AND RESERVES, 1993**
Excluding debt and unrealised equity gains

Per cent of end year assets

Source: OECD.

low credit ratings for their non-deposit liabilities and a high level of unprovisioned bad loans relative to operating profits (Figure 26).

...but problems persist elsewhere in the financial sector

Balance-sheet problems are more severe in the "second-tier" regional banks, credit and agricultural co-operatives[38] and non-bank credit institutions. While the first tier of regional banks (accounting for 17 per cent of total loans by private credit institutions) have strong local franchises and are generally sound financially, some of the second tier (which in total account for a further 7 per cent of loans) are much weaker and less well run. Most of these "second-tier" banks, which prior to 1989 were mutual savings associations, have been more affected by the deterioration of asset quality. Consequently, the proportion of their loans that are due to bankrupt companies is more than twice that of the major banks.[39] Indeed, 48 of the 65 banks in this category are more exposed to bankrupt companies than are the major banks on average (Figure 27). Five of these banks (with a total loan book of Y 6 trillion) have proportionately three times as much

Table 12. **Indicators of major banks' balance sheets**[1]

Trillion Yen

	March 1992	March 1993	March 1994	March 1995
Profit and loss account[2]				
Net operating profits	2.4	3.2	3.2	2.8
Specific loan provisions	0.5	0.9	1.4	1.6
Write-offs	0.1	0.2	0.2	0.7
Loss on debt sales to CCPC	0.0	0.2	1.8	1.5
Total bad loan charges	0.6	1.4	3.4	3.9
Security gains	0.8	0.0	1.8	3.1
Other charges[3]	0.2	0.5	0.8	1.8
Recurring profits[4]	2.0	1.3	0.8	0.2
Taxation	1.1	0.8	0.3	0.2
After tax profit[5]	0.9	0.5	0.5	–0.1
Balance sheet				
Non-performing loans (A)	8.0	12.8	13.6	12.5
To legally bankrupt companies	n.a.	2.0	2.3	2.6
Loans six months overdue	n.a.	10.8	11.3	9.9
Total loans (B)	396.5	395.9	388.1	381.3
(A/B, per cent)	2.0	3.2	3.5	3.3
Loan loss reserve (C)	1.0	1.9	3.0	4.3
(C/A, per cent)	13.1	14.6	22.3	34.3
Non-performing loans, net of provisions (D)	7.0	10.9	10.6	8.2
Unrealized securities gains (E)	17.3	17.8	20.4	9.0
Non-performing loans net of provisions relative to unrealized gains (D/E)	40.5	61.2	52.0	91.1
Memorandum items:				
Bank capital	. .	. .	. .	. .
Capital adequacy ratio[6]	8.27	9.31	9.71	8.92

1. The major banks include city banks, long-term credit banks and trust banks.
2. Net operating profits represent net interest income plus commissions and trading income less operating costs such as staff, depreciation etc. They are calculated before any provision for bad loan amortization.
3. Mainly general provisions against non-performing loans which are set at 0.3 per cent of outstanding loans.
4. Recurring profits are operating profits less total bad loan charges plus the gains arising from security sales less other charges.
5. After tax profit represents recurring profit less taxation.
6. This is calculated as an average of individual ratios weighted by the total assets of the banks.
Source: Federation of Bankers' Associations of Japan, *Analysis of Financial Statements of All Banks.*

Figure 26. **NON-PERFORMING LOANS NET OF PROVISIONS
RELATIVE TO OPERATING PROFITS OF MAJOR BANKS**

March 1995

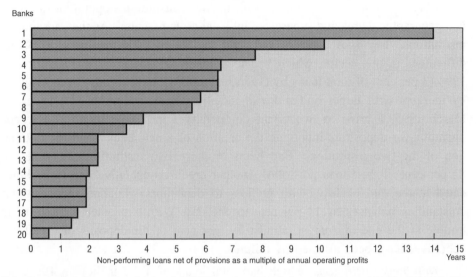

Note: One bank made an operating loss in FY 1994 and so the ratio has not been calculated for that bank. The individual banks are referenced by a number.
Source: Federation of Japanese Banks.

Figure 27. **TIER 2 REGIONAL BANKS: EXPOSURE TO BANKRUPT COMPANIES**

Per cent of all loans

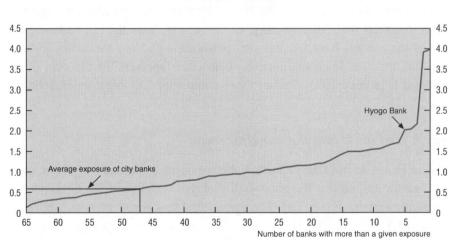

Source: Federation of Japanese Banks.

49

bankrupt debt on their books as the major banks and one of these five, the Hyogo Bank, had to be liquidated in the summer with no loss to depositors.

Credit co-operatives are non-profit financial institutions operating in a limited geographical area and supervised by local governments.[40] As they are mutual institutions, they take deposits and lend mainly to their members. Financial difficulties in this sector, which had total loans amounting to Y 19 trillion in 1994 (3 per cent of total loans by credit institutions), have usually been resolved by mergers with larger and more financially sound institutions. However, in March 1995, a crisis at two credit co-operatives in Tokyo required a rescue operation for depositors involving the creation of a new bank[41] and the liquidation of the two institutions. Bad loans of these two institutions amounted to 82 per cent of their loan portfolio. Another credit co-operative had to be liquidated at the end of July, with no loss to depositors who had reduced their outstanding balances by 14 per cent in one day. With two other institutions in trouble at the end of August, almost 7 1/2 per cent of the deposits of credit co-operatives have been affected by failures.

Non-bank institutions, which had total loans of Y 92 trillion in 1995, are active in lending in real estate, leasing and consumer finance markets. The greatest problem is the seven housing loan companies (HLCs), which represent 2 per cent of total loans by private credit institutions. These companies were formed by major financial institutions in the 1970s in order to meet the demand for housing loans at the time. As the major banks entered the residential loan market in the 1980s, the HLCs partly lost their original franchise and increased their commercial real estate lending. Consequently, with the fall in land prices, many of their assets have become non-performing and are backed by collateral worth less than the loan. On average, bad loans represent 74 per cent of their lending and, in June 1995, four of these companies had negative shareholders' equity.

...which feed back into the banking sector

The HLCs do not take deposits but have borrowed extensively from private credit institutions, so that the poor quality of their asset portfolio directly affects the banking system (Figure 28). The agricultural co-operatives, which have been the biggest lenders to the HLCs also have the largest proportionate exposure – much greater than that of trust banks (Figure 29). They appear to have become

Figure 28. **FUNDING SOURCES OF HOUSING LOAN COMPANIES**
June 1995

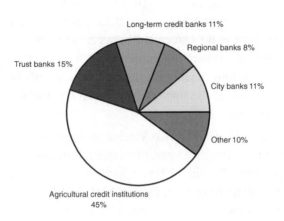

Source: Ministry of Finance.

Figure 29. **EXPOSURE TO HOUSING LOAN COMPANIES**
Per cent of all loans
June 1995

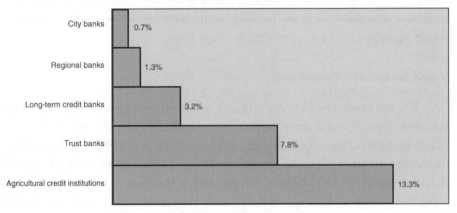

Source: Ministry of Finance and Bank of Japan.

involved in this type of lending from 1989 onwards. The major banks may face pressure to assume the debts of troubled HLCs, particularly those with which they have equity and lending linkages. However, the large number of lenders and owners associated with each HLC makes their restructuring more complicated, the more so since there is no agreement between agricultural co-operatives and parent banks about how to share the burden of such restructuring.[42] Existing loan restructuring plans put into place with the co-operation of the lending banks in 1993 thus far have reduced the interest paid by HLCs, but public recognition of the losses was postponed.

In March 1995, the CCPC also carried a large portfolio, initially worth Y 8.5 trillion, of non-performing loans purchased from major banks at an average discount of 55 per cent. By July 1995, it had bought a further Y 0.2 trillion of loans. These acquisitions have been financed by the banks granting loans to the CCPC at commercial rates of interest but with interest payments being initially capitalised. Despite the absence of interest payments, such bank loans to the CCPC (which, in March 1995, amounted to Y 3.8 trillion)[43] are not classified as non-performing. The CCPC has sold only Y 171 billion of collateral (4.5 per cent of its portfolio) since its establishment, reflecting a lack of purchasers for real estate at current prices. Commercial land prices in metropolitan areas have already fallen markedly, particularly in Tokyo, where they have halved since the peak in 1991 (Figure 30). However, rents have also declined, thus moderating the rise in the yield on office property. Moreover, the continued construction of buildings planned during the last expansion will further boost the vacancy rate, which has already risen significantly since 1993.

...and insurance companies

The life insurance industry – which is almost exclusively mutually owned – has also experienced a deterioration in its financial position in recent years. Its major problem comes from the fall in the total return on its assets – which are distributed between loans, bonds, equity and real estate investments (Figure 31) – from 6.4 per cent in FY 1990 to 3.8 per cent in the year to March 1994.[44] At that level, the return is below those that had been guaranteed on life and annuity policies, which were as high as 6 per cent.[45] The insurance companies also have about Y 0.5 trillion of non-performing loans (0.8 per cent of their loan portfolio). As in the banking system, the extent of the bad loan problems faced by different

Figure 30.   **THE REAL ESTATE MARKET**

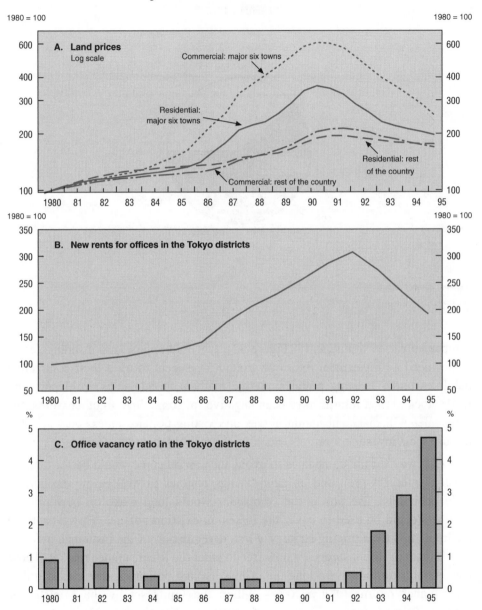

Source: National Land Agency, *Published Land Price;* Japan Building Owners and Managers Association, *Building Survey.*

53

Figure 31. **PORTFOLIO COMPOSITION OF LIFE INSURANCE COMPANIES**
February 1995

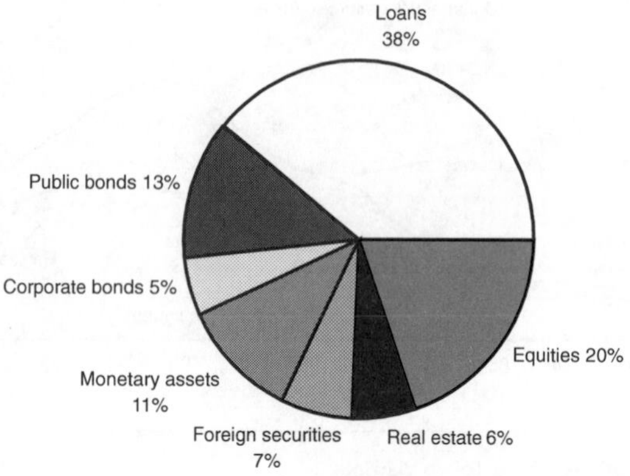

Loans
38%

Public bonds 13%

Corporate bonds 5%

Monetary assets
11%

Foreign securities
7%

Real estate 6%

Equities 20%

Source: Bank of Japan.

companies varies significantly (Figure 32). It would appear that insurance companies need an investment return of around 5 per cent to meet their contractual liabilities under existing policies. At the moment, bond yields are 3 per cent, while stock market returns have been negative for some time. In other words, the companies will make substantial losses on existing policies unless they are able to raise their investment returns. Such losses would jeopardise their capital base.

One way for the companies to avoid such an outcome would be for them to lower the returns promised on new savings policies to well below the current yield on bonds. The profits the companies would then make on new savings contracts could be used to cover the losses on existing policies. However, there are limits to such a pricing strategy. *First,* deregulation of the insurance industry means that non-life insurers are now free to enter the life insurance market. These new entrants do not have a long tail of loss-making policies and so can afford to offer higher returns to investors – within the limits set by the Ministry of Finance. *Second,* consumers may prefer to invest directly in bonds if returns on new insurance policies are reduced too much. These limits suggest that life insurance companies will not be able to fully offset losses on existing policies

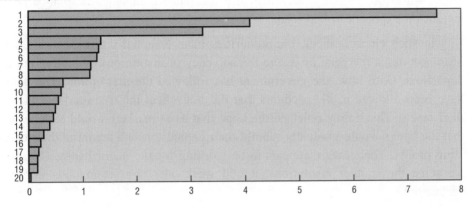

Figure 32. BAD LOAN EXPOSURE OF 20 MAJOR LIFE INSURANCE COMPANIES

Percentage of total loans, March 1994

Insurance companies[1]

1. Individual insurance companies are referenced by a number.
Source: Balance Sheet Data.

and may come under increasing financial pressure. The fall in the rate of return on assets has affected private pension funds as well, which are still being valued on the basis of a nominal return of $5\frac{1}{2}$ per cent, suggesting that these schemes are underfunded and will require higher contribution rates.

...thus stressing the need for further measures to recapitalise the financial industry

The Ministry of Finance has now recognised that the extent of the problems facing Japanese financial institutions goes well beyond the Y 13 trillion of bad loans declared by the 21 major banks. However, disclosure of information on the health of the secondary banking system – accounting for half of total bank loans – is fragmentary. The few data available suggest that the credit problems there are worse than in the major banks whereas the official estimates appear to assume that the problem is similar. The overall position, moreover, masks particularly difficult situations at certain institutions or groups of institutions. As noted, some trust banks are particularly badly hit, while the poor quality of the loans held by HLCs poses problems for the agricultural credit co-operatives. The second tier of regional banks also contains a number of institutions whose health is fragile. Moreover, many of these secondary institutions do not appear to be earning the operating profits necessary for a quick resolution of the problem by their own efforts. Finally, as noted, life insurance companies have incurred a significant exposure to bad loans.

In such circumstances, the authorities have essentially three options: for-bearance; assist mergers; or ensure the solvency of institutions by bailing out all depositors. Until now, the government has followed the first option. The banks have been allowed to file accounts that did not reflect the true market value of their assets. This policy reflected the hope that asset markets would recover and that the banks would gradually rebuild their capital through retaining their oper-ating profits. The strategy appears to be working for the major banks. However for some the smaller institutions, it will work only if asset markets improve substantially.

To deal with cases where forbearance is not applicable, the government has historically relied on assisted mergers. This approach implies that a major bank, usually with some link to the troubled institution, assumes the assets and liabili-ties of the latter. Alternatively, the bank will finance a new institution to which the assets and liabilities are transferred, sometimes with aid from the Deposit Insurance Corporation (DIC) or the Bank of Japan. Such a policy worked well while the troubled institutions were small in relation to the major banks and the resources of the DIC. However, the DIC does not have the funds to deal with all of the current problem areas and the major banks need time to solve their own difficulties. This has led to an erosion of the support given by parent banks to subsidiaries. As some of the most troubled financial institutions have no parent bank, at the moment the scope for complete resolution of the problem using assisted mergers is small.

In June 1995, the Ministry of Finance announced a five-year package addressing the banks' balance-sheet problem. It stressed that the Deposit Insur-ance Corporation will ensure that all deposits in troubled banks are honoured, subject to four conditions: the resignation of the management of the bank; burden sharing with the equity owners; rationalisation of the bank; and a search for alternative forms of financial assistance. In addition, the government announced that, within six to twelve months, it will decide on guidelines to resolve the bad loans problem and, within five years, it will establish a framework for financial stability involving increased self-responsibility for depositors. Intervention by the

Bank of Japan, beyond its role in resolving liquidity crises, would be limited to cases where systemic risks cannot be avoided. Finally, the government established a Financial System Stabilisation Committee which produced an interim report in September on the basic principles for the disposition of failing or failed financial institutions.

Following on from this report, the government decided to tackle the problem of non-performing loans by first undertaking a survey of all financial institutions to determine the extent of bad loans. Moreover, the government will introduce legislation, in the next regular session of the Diet, to enable it to take measures to correct mismanagement and dispose of the assets of failed or failing financial institutions at an earlier stage. The legislation will also create a transparent framework for the use of private sector capital in such asset disposals and will allow the deposit insurance rate to be increased. In the case of the HLCs, the government intends to agree with the concerned parties a specific plan to dispose of their assets by the end of 1995. This may involve the creation of a new institution which will purchase the loans of the HLCs. At the same time, the government is considering the use of public funds, on a temporary basis, to help the orderly disposal of the assets of failed financial institutions.

The use of public funds to cope with the problems of troubled financial institutions – the remaining option to safeguard the solvency of these institutions and so protect depositors – could take different forms. The government might channel finance directly from the general account of central or local government budgets. Alternatively, it could use the DIC,[46] the Savings Deposit Insurance Corporation (SDIC),[47] institutions under the Fiscal Investment and Loan Programme (FILP), the Bank of Japan, or create a new institution to purchase the real estate collateral of ailing banks. According to the usual practice, proceeding off-budget, *i.e.* through the above-mentioned institutions, would not involve an increase in conventionally-measured government debt. Indeed, only two of these institutions, the DIC and the SDIC, have a source of income (deposit insurance premia) other than the government to cover its borrowing costs. The other institutions would have to either rely on increased subsidies from the government or reduce their payments to it. Thus, in practice, the use of the off-budget channel would have similar effects on public finances in the long term.

Therefore, the fundamental choice is not so much whether to operate on or off the budget but rather to what extent general taxation should be used to fund the cost of the bailout as opposed to raising deposit insurance rates. While general taxation has a broader base and the society, as a whole, will gain from a healthier banking system, it can be argued that banks and depositors benefit from a deposit guarantee and so should expect to pay the associated costs. In any case, equity considerations would have to influence the way to proceed. In particular, deposit-insurance premia might have to be linked to the riskiness of financial institutions. There are, of course, other considerations in play: the decision to use off-budget funds can be taken quicker and without parliamentary approval, whereas the use of the government budget requires the approval of parliament or local assemblies.

Given the continued decline in commercial land prices, a delay in resolving the financial sector's bad debt problem will increase its eventual size. A quicker resolution of the problem would require the restoration of a better-functioning real estate market that would lead to greater sales of collateral assets. Over the longer term, Japanese banks will need to improve their profitability, which is the lowest amongst the major seven countries (Figure 33), which will likely require a reduction in operating costs in the banking system.

Figure 33. **INTERNATIONAL COMPARISON OF BANK PROFITABILITY**[1]

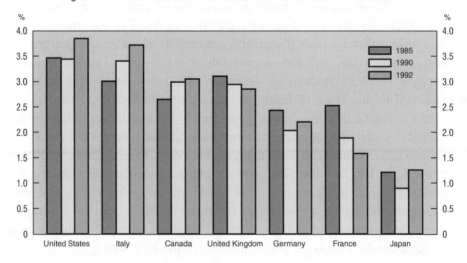

1. Ratio of net interest income to average assets for commercial banks.
Source: OECD.

The fiscal stance

After the 1994 budget stimulus

The FY 1994 budget stimulated household demand as the result of an across-the-board income tax cut (Table 13). The tax refunds, combined with the weak economy, reduced total revenues by 7 per cent from the previous year. Two supplementary budgets pushed up public works spending by an additional Y 1.6 trillion in FY 1994. The first was to help the agricultural sector adjust to the Uruguay Round trade agreement, while the second was to support the reconstruction of the Kobe area after the earthquake. Despite these additional outlays, total spending in FY 1994 was 2 per cent lower than in the previous year. As a result, the central government deficit changed little from 1993. However, fiscal policy remained expansionary as actual public works expenditure continued to increase, reflecting delays in implementation of previous supplementary budgets.

The central government deficit should rise in 1995

The initial budget for FY 1995 projects total revenues to be 3 per cent higher than the estimated outcome for FY 1994 (Table 13), despite an income tax cut equal to the previous year's reduction. The income tax structure was changed in FY 1995 in a way which benefited middle-income groups. In order to keep the overall tax cuts at the same level as in FY 1994, the uniform percentage reduction in tax payments was prolonged but at a lower rate. On the spending side, the initial FY 1995 budget is 3 per cent below the previous year, despite a 4 per cent rise in public works expenditure. However, this comparison exaggerates the tightness of the policy stance of the budget, since FY 1994 expenditures were boosted by the early repayment of certain loans. If these outlays are excluded, government spending in the FY 1995 initial budget would be stable. In addition, the government introduced a supplementary budget in May 1995 to finance rebuilding in the Kobe area and increased lending to small and medium-sized enterprises.

A second supplementary budget was introduced in October to implement the new economic package announced in September 1995 to provide further support to activity. This package – the fifth since 1992 – totalled Y 14.2 trillion (3.1 per cent of GDP) and included Y 9.1 trillion for public investment and disaster relief, Y 3.2 trillion for the advance purchase of land and Y 1.9 trillion for housing

Table 13. Central government budget

| | FY 1993 Settlement | Trillion yen | | | | | | | | | Per cent Increase FY 1995 compared with FY 1994 | |
| | | FY 1994 | | | | FY 1995 | | | | | | |
		Initial budget	First supplementary budget	Second supplementary budget	Total budget	Initial budget	First supplementary budget	Second supplementary budget	Total budget	Initial budget	Total budget
Total expenditure	**75.1**	**73.1**	**-0.7**	**1.0**	**73.4**	**71.0**	**2.7**	**5.3**	**79.0**	**-2.9**	**7.6**
General spending	43.6	40.9	0.7	1.0	42.6	42.1	2.7	5.1	49.9	3.1	17.0
of which: Public works	10.0	7.8	1.0	0.7	9.4	8.1	1.4	3.5	13.1	4.6	40.0
Debt servicing[1]	13.7	14.4	-0.7	0.0	13.6	13.2	0.0	-0.3	12.9	-7.9	-4.8
Transfers to local government	13.9	12.8	-0.7	0.0	12.1	13.2	0.0		13.2	3.6	9.5
NTT redemption[2]	2.6	2.3			2.3	1.1			1.1	-51.0	-51.0
Other expenditure	1.3	2.8			2.8	1.3		0.6	1.9	-54.3	-34.3
Total revenue	61.6	59.4	-1.9	-0.6	56.9	58.4	-0.1	0.6	58.9	-1.8	2.3
Taxes	54.1	53.7	-2.2	-0.6	50.8	53.7	-0.1	0.0	53.6	0.1	5.5
Non-tax revenue[3]	7.4	5.8	0.3	0.0	6.1	4.7	0.0	0.6	5.3	-19.3	-13.1
Deficit[4]	16.2	13.6	1.3	1.6	16.5	12.6	2.8	4.7	20.1	-7.7	22.0
Construction bonds	16.2	10.5	1.1	0.8	12.3	9.7	2.3	4.5	16.5	-7.3	23.7
Other bonds	0.0	3.1	0.2	0.8	4.1	2.9	0.6	0.2	3.6	-9.0	-12.5
Memorandum:											
Expenditure excluding NTT redemption[5]	70.0	68.6	-0.7	1.0	68.9	68.8	2.7	5.3	76.8	0.3	11.5

1. Including the repayment of maturing debt.
2. Redemption of the NTT special loans made to Industrial Investment Special Account.
3. The figure of FY 1993 includes transfer from settlement adjustment account.
4. The deficit is equal to the gross issuance of government debt.
5. Includes NTT redemption included in debt servicing.
Source: Ministry of Finance.

loans and credits to small businesses. As a result, total spending should rise by 7 per cent including a 40 per cent increase in public works expenditure (Table 13). Overall, the central government deficit is now officially projected to reach Y 20 trillion (4.3 per cent of GDP) in FY 1995, up from an estimated Y 16.5 trillion in FY 1994.

...and local authority deficits will also increase

The deterioration of the financial position of local authorities is expected to continue in FY 1995 as, in the initial budgets, the growth of expenditure (excluding debt service) is projected to accelerate to 4 per cent despite a slowdown in capital spending (Table 14). With revenues stagnating for the second consecutive year, total local government borrowing, including that of local public corporations and other special account activities, is projected to reach Y 16 trillion in FY 1995, a figure equivalent to 3.4 per cent of GDP.

...resulting in a further deterioration of the general government position

The combined central government and local authority deficit, which rose by 2.5 per cent of GDP on a national accounts basis in FY 1994, is projected to increase by a further 0.5 per cent to reach 7.7 per cent of GDP in FY 1995 (Table 15). With the social security surplus[48] projected to remain stable at around 3.5 per cent of GDP, the general government financial deficit may rise from 3.6 per cent in FY 1994 to about 4¹/₄ per cent this fiscal year. After allowing for the effects of cyclical changes in economic activity on the budget, the structural deficit of the general government is projected by the OECD Secretariat at close to 2¹/₄ per cent of GDP in FY 1995, corroborating the impression of a more stimulatory fiscal stance this year.

The large government budget deficit has led to a rapid increase in the stock of public debt relative to GDP, reversing the significant progress in fiscal consolidation which took place between 1987 and 1991 (Figure 34). According to OECD Secretariat projections, the ratio of general government gross debt to GDP is expected to rise to about 95 per cent in 1995, significantly above the OECD average. In contrast, *net debt* should remain relatively low compared with the rest of the OECD area, reflecting the substantial assets of the social security system.

Table 14. **Local authority budget**

Fiscal years

	Billion yen			Per cent	
	1993	1994	1995	1994	1995
General account					
Revenues					
Local taxes	34 555	32 581	33 764	−5.7	3.6
Local transfer taxes	1 951	1 926	1 987	−1.3	3.1
Local allocation taxes	15 435	15 502	16 153	0.4	4.2
Subsidies from national government	12 229	14 174	12 802	15.9	−9.7
Rent and fees	1 335	1 414	1 450	5.9	2.5
Miscellaneous	4 684	4 939	5 050	5.5	2.2
Total	70 189	70 537	71 204	0.5	0.9
Expenditure					
Wages and salaries	21 900	22 330	22 698	2.0	1.6
Administration	15 908	16 111	16 817	1.3	4.4
Debt service[1]	6 554	8 922	7 694	36.1	−13.8
Repairs	867	895	917	3.2	2.4
Capital expenditure	26 794	29 072	30 362	8.5	4.4
Others	4 394	3 598	4 021	−18.1	11.8
Total	76 415	80 928	82 509	5.9	2.0
Deficit of general account[2]	6 225	10 392	11 305		
Public corporations and other borrowing	4 104	4 342	4 728		
Total borrowing	10 359	14 734	16 033		
As per cent of GDP	2.2	3.1	3.4		
Financed by					
Borrowing from FILP	5 700	6 500	7 250		
Specific purpose loans from government	11	0	0		
Local public enterprises borrowing	1 455	1 660	1 850		
Market borrowing	880	1 200	1 400		
Private placements	2 313	5 374	5 533		

1. An unknown part of this represents debt redemption.
2. The deficit is equal to newly issued local bonds in the general account.
Source: Ministry of Finance and Economic Planning Agency.

Table 15. **General government financial balances**

Deficit (−), surplus (+) as percentage of GDP
Fiscal years

	1990	1991	1992	1993	1994	1995
Central government	−0.3	−0.2	−2.2	−2.9	−3.7	−3.9
Local authorities	0.3	−0.1	−1.1	−1.7	−3.4	−3.7
Central and local governments	−0.0	−0.3	−3.3	−4.6	−7.1	−7.7
Social security	3.6	3.8	3.4	3.5	3.5	3.5
General government	3.5	3.5	0.1	−1.1	−3.6	−4.2
of which:						
Cyclical component	2.0	2.5	0.3	0.8	−0.9	−1.9
Structural component	1.6	1.0	−0.2	−1.9	−2.7	−2.3

Source: EPA, *Annual Report on National Accounts* and OECD.

Classification by policy objectives of the FILP[5]

Housing	26.2	25.4	30.3	29.5	33.5	35.3
Environment, water and sewerage	14.1	15.7	15.3	16.6	16.4	16.4
Welfare	3.5	2.9	3.1	3.8	3.7	4.0
Education	4.4	3.6	2.0	1.8	2.1	2.0
Small and medium-sized enterprises	18.7	18.0	15.7	14.6	14.9	15.3
Agriculture, forestry and fisheries	4.9	4.3	3.2	2.5	2.5	2.9
Land conservation and disaster reconstruction	1.7	2.3	1.2	1.5	1.2	1.3
Roads	5.7	8.8	9.8	9.9	8.8	7.8
Transportation and communication	9.6	8.5	8.3	7.9	5.6	4.6
Regional development	2.6	2.4	2.5	2.7	2.7	2.6
Industrial and technological development	3.0	2.9	2.9	3.5	3.3	3.1
Trade and economic co-operation	5.6	5.3	5.8	5.8	5.1	4.7
Total	100.0	100.0	100.0	100.0	100.0	100.0

1. Fiscal Investment and Loan Program.
2. The figures of FY 1980, FY 1985 and FY 1990 were actual. The figures from FY 1993 to FY 1995 were from the initial plans.
3. Estimated by using the outstandings of FILP.
4. The figure of FY 1995 is estimated by OECD.
5. All figures were from the initial plans, excluding portfolio investment.
Source: Ministry of Finance.

...especially if the FILP program is taken into account

As noted in previous Surveys, about half of the social security surpluses are placed with the Fiscal Investment and Loan Program (FILP), with the remainder invested in financial markets (see the 1993 Survey). The FILP also receives deposits and loans from the postal savings and insurance system as well as funds borrowed from capital markets. However, a significant source of FILP resources is the repayment of previous loans made by the FILP (Table 16). As a result, the gross FILP budget, a management allocation tool, overstates the importance of the FILP as a source of new credit for the economy which is better measured by the change in the net outstanding FILP balances.

The two principal purposes of FILP expenditures are to finance local authorities and public corporations directly and to channel funds to the private sector through lending by government-affiliated financial institutions. During 1993 and 1994, the FILP budget has been stable at around 6 per cent of GDP, excluding repayments of previous loans. In the initial budget for FY 1995, the government plans to stabilise net lending by the FILP. Credits to the public sector will fall by

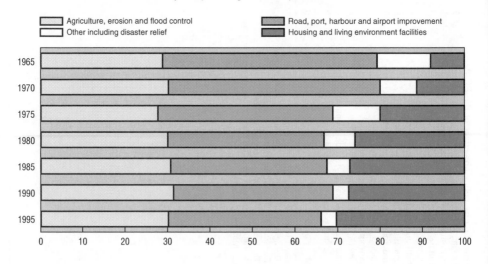

Figure 35. **PUBLIC WORKS EXPENDITURE: THE SHARE OF DIFFERENT PROGRAMMES**
Fiscal years; percentage of total expenditure

Source: Ministry of Finance.

4 per cent as a result of reduced lending to public corporations.[49] In contrast, lending to the private sector, primarily housing and small businesses, is projected to rise. Since the FILP consists of financial institutions whose assets and liabilities balance, its budget does not increase the net debt of the public sector. FILP operations do, though, allow public corporations (outside the general government sector) to accumulate net debt without the direct issuance of bonds on the capital markets (these corporations had deficits of 0.2 per cent of GDP in FY 1993). They also limit the dependence of local authorities on the bond market.

The FILP will play a major role in the government's Y 630 trillion public investment plan for the ten years FY 1995 to FY 2004. This plan replaces the FY 1991 to FY 2000 programme, which envisaged the expenditure of Y 430 trillion. It requires an annual average increase in public investment spending of about 5 per cent between FY 1992[50] and FY 2004. In practice, however, given the significant growth of public investment during FY 1993 and FY 1994 and, notwithstanding falls at the end of 1994 and beginning of 1995, the increase in this expenditure category from now on may be somewhat less. The major objective of the plan is to enhance the quality of life. As a result, investment to improve the living environment and support welfare and cultural activities should increase slightly to between 60 and 65 per cent of total outlays. For some ministries, however, the share in central government public works spending has changed little over the past 30 years despite rapid adjustments in the industrial structure of the economy. For instance, in 1995, public works expenditure to improve agricultural production conditions, the rural environment and flood control accounted for the same proportion of total spending (about 30 per cent) as in 1965, though the share devoted to the rural environment increased substantially (Figure 35).

III. Progress in deregulation

Deregulation has been a major objective of the Japanese Government during the past few years. Reducing government intervention in the economy is intended: *a)* to increase output by creating new business opportunities, a particularly important goal given the poor performance of the economy since 1991; *b)* to narrow the price differentials between Japan and other countries; and *c)* to facilitate the expansion of imports and thus ease friction with major trading partners. In practice, the deregulation process has been driven by the numerous liberalisation packages introduced by the Japanese Government as well as by the negotiations with the United States under the *Japan-United States Framework for a New Economic Partnership.*

This chapter first reviews deregulation initiatives since 1994 before discussing the most recent package announced in March 1995. It then summarises the measures stemming from the US-Japan framework talks. The deregulation of the distribution sector is examined in more detail in the next chapter.

Progress since 1994

The government has announced numerous deregulation plans during the past two years, including: *The Emergency Economic Package* (September 1993); *Policy for the Promotion of Administrative Reform* (February 1994); and *The Policy for Promoting Reform Hereafter* (July 1994). Together these contained 1 213 proposals, of which about four-fifths had been implemented by the end of 1994 (Table 17). Another significant step was the implementation of the Administrative Procedures Law in October 1994 followed, in 1995, by a plan to rationalise public corporations.

Table 17. **The implementation of past deregulation plans**

As of 15 December 1994

		Emergency Economic Package (September 1993)	Policy for promoting Administrative Reform (February 1994)	Regarding the Policy for Promoting Deregulation Hereafter (July 1994)	Total
Measures for which the implementation deadline has already arrived	Total	74	484	66	624
	Already implemented	74	482	65	621
	To be implemented	0	2	1	3
Measures for which the implementation deadline has *not* yet already arrived	Total	33	314	242	589
	Already implemented	19	241	69	329
	To be implemented[1]	14	73	173	260

1. Of the 260 measures in this category, 252 are still under discussion.
Source: Management and Coordination Agency.

The July 1994 package

The July 1994 package targeted regulations related to housing and land, information and telecommunications, market access and the distribution system, and the financial system.

Housing and land

Measures in this area were focused on improving the efficiency of land use. The transfer of agricultural land in urban areas to residential use is being promoted and the process has been made more transparent. The redevelopment of areas around railway stations has been encouraged, while the waiting time for approval to build has been shortened. Acceptance of foreign test and evaluation data on building materials has been increased in order to boost imports and reduce costs.

Information and telecommunications

The procedures for granting domestic broadcasting licenses and increasing the number of destinations of international value-added networks were simplified. In addition, the guidelines for the on-line transfer of funds were clarified. The process of gaining approval for telecommunications equipment was modified. There has also been progress in the mobile phone market. Competition has been increased by introducing seven carriers in each regional market and separating mobile telecommunication services from Nippon Telegraph and Telephone. This has led to a significant fall in the cost of cellular phone services and a doubling in the number of subscribers in the year to March 1995.

Market access improvement and the distribution sector

Acceptance of foreign certification and inspection data was increased to promote imports of products such as food and pharmaceuticals, and new customs procedures were introduced. The regulation of warehouses and their fee structure has been relaxed, while the geographic limits on the construction of new petrol stations have been eased. The Transport Ministry decided to allow airlines to reduce their fares by as much as 50 per cent without requiring prior approval. In addition, the Diet passed bills easing controls on the activities of foreign lawyers in Japan[51] and establishing a new product liability law.[52] The government also introduced bills to liberalise imports of petroleum products, such as gasoline, and to encourage new entries to the wholesale electricity business.

The financial system

Regulations on interest rates and the length of home loans offered by banks were abolished in July 1994. This resulted in an immediate 50 basis-point drop in interest rates and a wider variety of loans. In addition, the liberalisation of interest rates on non-time deposits was completed in October 1994. Financial institutions were allowed to engage in forward rate agreements and forward exchange agreements, thus allowing traders to hedge against unexpected changes in interest rates and exchange rates. Additional changes in financial services and insurance made in the context of the framework talks with the United States are discussed below.

The Administrative Procedures Law

The Administrative Procedures Law (APL) is an attempt to make the bureaucratic decision-making process more transparent and less arbitrary. It imposed uniform rules on the processing of applications, the handling of disputes and the practice of administrative guidance. Every ministry and agency now must publicly set clear schedules and deadlines for processing applications and will no longer be able to refuse to accept applications. Judgements are to be based on concrete criteria and negative decisions must be explained, giving affected parties the opportunity to present their views. Finally, the APL limits the use of administrative guidance (*gyoseishido*), a major source of bureaucratic power.[53] Ministries and agencies are required to indicate clearly and publicly the purpose and intent of any guidance. Since such guidance does not have the force of law, retaliation will not be permitted against companies that choose not to follow the government's advice. Another objective of the APL is to bring Japan's bureaucratic standards and procedures more into line with other countries, thus helping to ease trade frictions and to attract foreign investment.

The APL excludes many important areas, such as police and public safety activities, tax and customs procedures, patent applications and immigration and naturalisation matters. In addition, it does not provide any sanction against bureaucrats who violate the new law. Despite these limitations, the application of the APL thus far suggests that it can be an important tool in changing bureaucratic procedures and limiting government intervention in the economy.

Reform of government corporations

The government outlined a plan in January 1995 to reform 92 government corporations that have been criticised for inefficiency and a lack of accountability. This plan raised concern, though, about a loss of jobs resulting from the closure or merger of these institutions. Specific proposals were announced in February to merge fourteen government corporations into seven, while eliminating or privatising five others. The only action decided thus far is the merger of the Export Import Bank of Japan and the Overseas Economic Co-operation Fund in four years.

The March 1995 deregulation plan

The latest government programme, announced in March 1995, incorporated a more transparent deregulation process. In preparing this package, the government solicited comments from interested parties and received replies from 165 organisations, including six governments and the European Union.[54] In addition, a preliminary form of the package was presented for public comment in early March before it was finalised. There was a high degree of overlap between the proposals made by domestic businesses and those from overseas, reflecting perhaps the internationalisation of Japanese firms. Of the 1 750 deregulation proposals received, about 750 had already been implemented or were already included in previous deregulation packages. Another 350 are still under consideration, while 450 were regarded as too difficult to implement.[55] The package also established a process of continuous regulatory review to ensure that it is updated in line with changing economic and social conditions. It will be reviewed each December on the basis of proposals from foreign and domestic companies, as well as foreign governments, and a revised plan will be presented the following March.[56] Measures taken as a result of negotiations with foreign governments will be added to the package. In addition, the new plan includes a timetable indicating the date by when each measure is to be implemented. Originally announced as a five-year programme, the government decided in response to the sharp rise in the yen in April to compress it to three years. Finally, the government will also prepare a white paper on deregulation each year to inform the public about progress in implementing the package.

Concretely, the package contains 1 091 proposals covering eleven areas (Table 18). A summary of these proposals is provided in Annex 1. The piecemeal nature of deregulation is reflected by the fact that most of these areas were

Table 18. **The March 1995 deregulation package**

Proposals by subject

Housing and land	86
Information and telecommunications	53
Distribution	120
Transportation	168
Standards, certification and import processing	240
Financial services and insurance	83
Energy	26
Employment and labour	30
Environmental protection	15
Public safety and disaster prevention	131
Other	139
Total	1 091

Source: Management and Coordination Agency.

addressed in previous deregulation plans. Although the package is based on the principle of eliminating economic regulation, some of the measures tend to be vague and imprecise. The package includes commitments to study certain regulations without indicating what action, if any, will be taken at the end of the review.

The package is accompanied by changes to increase the effectiveness of competition policy to ensure that the benefits of easing regulation are not offset by restrictive business practices or administrative guidance from the government. The Japan Fair Trade Commission (JFTC) has established guidelines to ensure that administrative guidance does not lead to practices which are in conflict with the Anti-Monopoly Act. Laws which allow exemptions from the Act for certain practices, including cartels, will be reviewed with the intention of abolishing such exemptions in principle by March 1999. The JFTC will also review, by March 1998, the remaining areas where retail price maintenance is permitted, as well as the notification system for mergers, while beginning a study of the regulation on holding companies. Finally, the JFTC will be strengthened in order to provide more vigorous efforts to ensure fair competition.

The Japan-United States Framework for a New Economic Partnership

As a result of consultations under the so-called "framework talks", which were established in July 1993 (see 1994 Survey), Japan and the United States have decided to implement measures in eight areas – financial services, insurance, government procurement of telecommunications and medical technology, patents, flat glass, autos and auto parts, as well as inward direct investment and buyer-supplier relationships. The objective is to address sectoral and structural issues related to international trade and investment. Assessment of the implementation of these measures, as well as the evaluation of the progress achieved, will be based on qualitative and quantitative criteria, which do not constitute numerical targets.

Each of the measures is based on the "Most-Favoured Nation" (MFN) principle, thereby allowing the increased opportunities to sell in the Japanese market to benefit all countries. The increase in exports to Japan resulting from previous measures taken by Japan and the United States following bilateral consultations have been shared by many countries (Table 19). The US share of Japanese imports of pharmaceuticals, medical instruments and citrus fruits all declined following bilateral talks in these areas. US producers did significantly increase their shares of Japanese imports of beef[57] and auto parts. The latter may reflect ''reverse imports'' from the more than 200 Japanese auto part companies operating in the United States. Actions taken in each of the eight areas as a result of the framework talks are briefly summarised below.

Financial services

The centre-piece of the financial services measures announced in January 1995 was the granting of partial access to public pension funds with assets of Y 100 trillion to both foreign and domestic investment advisory companies.[58] Previously, only trust banks and life insurance companies could manage this money. In the investment trust market (equivalent to US mutual funds), recent reforms will make it easier for foreign firms to enter and to operate in Japan. Finally, Japan will encourage disclosure of data on the performance of investment trust managers on a current market-value basis.[59]

The second major change is an increase in the transparency of financial regulation in line with the APL. The government announced an easing of restrictions on the introduction of new financial instruments and will respond to such requests promptly in writing. In addition, Japan will eliminate remaining barriers on cross border transactions. For example, foreign firms are now able to sell Euroyen bonds in Japan as soon as they are issued offshore rather than being forced to wait 90 days. In exchange, the United States announced it will continue national treatment[60] of Japanese firms providing financial services in the US market.[61]

Insurance

In October 1994, Japan announced measures to increase the transparency of regulations on the insurance industry and to strengthen competition policy in this area. A three-stage liberalisation of the approval process for insurance products and rates, consistent with appropriate protection of policyholders, is also planned. Moreover, a recent amendment of the Insurance Business Law, the first revision in 56 years, will introduce a broker system, which would allow agents to offer policies from competing firms rather than being limited to one company.[62] This is

Table 19. **Japan's imports of selected products covered by bilateral US-Japan consultations**

Industry/Country	Japanese imports ($ million)				Market share (per cent)	
	Year prior to the measures	1993	Change	Percentage change	Year prior to the measures	1993
Pharmaceuticals [1]						
United States	566.6	972.4	405.8	71.6	43.9	24.7
Germany	199.5	927.8	728.3	365.1	15.4	23.6
United Kingdom	63.2	433.2	370.0	585.4	4.9	11.0
Sweden	131.5	308.6	177.1	134.7	10.2	7.9
Medical instruments [1]						
United States	118.3	607.2	488.9	413.3	64.8	54.7
Germany	23.0	138.2	115.2	500.9	12.6	12.5
Singapore	1.2	78.3	77.1	6 425.0	0.7	7.1
Ireland	1.6	39.0	37.4	2 337.5	0.9	3.5
Wood products [2]						
Indonesia	1 067.1	1 729.3	662.2	62.1	66.2	59.8
Malaysia	54.6	351.7	297.1	544.1	3.4	12.2
United States	87.3	184.3	97.0	111.1	5.4	6.4
Canada	26.8	123.0	96.2	359.0	1.7	4.3
Auto parts [3]						
United States	72.4	357.2	284.8	393.4	29.5	34.1
Germany	71.1	194.7	123.6	173.8	29.0	18.6
Taiwan	7.8	86.1	78.3	1 003.8	3.2	8.2
Italy	22.1	69.6	47.5	214.9	9.0	6.7
Beef [4]						
United States	380.9	1 358.7	977.8	256.7	47.6	55.6
Australia	364.2	1 017.0	652.8	179.2	45.5	41.6
New Zealand	27.5	55.9	28.4	103.3	3.4	2.3
Canada	1.7	7.4	5.7	335.3	0.2	0.3
Citrus fruit [4]						
United States	286.6	362.7	76.1	26.6	92.5	79.2
Brazil	15.3	64.0	48.7	318.3	4.9	14.0
Israel	5.0	12.5	7.5	150.0	1.6	2.7

1. 1986 report on the "Market-Oriented Sector Selective" (MOSS) talks. Table shows the change from 1985 to 1993 in Japanese imports of SITC categories 54 (pharmaceuticals) and 872 (medical instruments).
2. 1990 measures. Table shows the change from 1989 to 1993 in Japanese imports of SITC category 63 (excluding 633).
3. 1987 report on the "Market-Oriented Sector Selective" (MOSS) talks. Table shows the change from 1986 to 1993 in Japanese imports of SITC category 784.
4. 1988 measures. Table shows the change from 1987 to 1993 in Japanese imports of SITC categories 0111 (beef), 0572 and 05851 (oranges and orange juice) and 05852 (grapefruit juice).
Source: OECD.

expected to boost competition and provide consumers with objective advice on insurance. In addition, this amendment will allow life and non-life insurance firms to enter each other's business fields.[63]

Government procurement of telecommunications and medical technology

In November 1994, Japan announced changes in its public procurement procedures for telecommunication products and services and medical technology in order to expand opportunities for sales by competitive foreign firms. An "overall greatest value" bid evaluation system, which takes into account other factors besides price, will be introduced so that sophisticated technology, both foreign and domestic, will not automatically be excluded because of its expense. In telecommunications, where government purchases totalled Y 62 billion in 1994,[64] early and detailed information on procurement plans will be provided. Both foreign and domestic firms will be allowed to comment on purchase plans before tenders are finalised and international standards will be used as much as possible. In addition, the number of single-source contracts, which tend to go primarily to Japanese companies, will be reduced.[65] Procedural changes in public purchasing methods have also been made in the field of medical technology, a Y 68 billion government procurement market in 1994. In addition, a comprehensive complaint mechanism and procedures for handling unfair bids will be established in this area as well as telecommunications.

Patents

Japan and the United States decided, in 1994, to take measures to harmonise their respective patent systems in order to improve intellectual property right protection in the two countries. The Japanese Patent Office will make four significant changes by the beginning of 1996. *First*, it has accepted initial patent filings in English since July 1995, provided a Japanese translation is submitted within two months. *Second*, firms that have submitted a patent application to a foreign government will be able to request accelerated examination for a corresponding patent filed in Japan beginning in 1996. Such applications will be processed within three years. The long examination period may have posed a problem for high technology firms that face short product life cycles and often rely on technological innovations for a competitive edge.[66] *Third*, the right of competing firms to file oppositions before a patent is granted will be abolished by January 1996. Under the new rules, only post grant oppositions will be considered.[67] *Fourth*, the power of government arbitration to force patent holders to license their technology to holders of dependent patents (which utilise another person's invention) has been limited since July 1995. Although this rule has been rarely used in recent years, it may have discouraged some inventors from filing for patents in Japan. In addition, the United States will also make significant changes in its patent system.[68]

Flat glass

Japan and the United States decided in December 1994 to implement measures in the market for flat glass where the US claimed the existence of exclusionary relationships between the three major producers[69] and the approximately 400 primary wholesalers. A JFTC survey in June 1993 found no violation of the Anti-Monopoly Act. It pointed out, however, that each manufacturer had established a parallel marketing channel composed primarily of *de facto* exclusive agents, making the market highly oligopolistic and discouraging new suppliers from entering the market. The JFTC also noted that this arrangement has facilitated ''concerted conduct'' among the producers and made some wholesalers reluctant to handle imported products, fearing that it would adversely affect their relationships with the manufacturers. Japan, on the other hand, claimed that foreign flat glass suppliers had not made sufficient sales and promotion efforts to enter the Japanese market, as reported in a MITI survey.

To alleviate these concerns, the Flat Glass Wholesalers Association of Japan publicly announced, in December 1994, that its members would broaden their supply bases to include additional foreign and domestic manufacturers, regardless of their capital affiliation. The major manufacturers responded by affirming that distributors are free to handle flat glass made by any company, foreign or domestic. The Japanese Government will monitor the market with a voluntary survey of wholesalers each year to determine the percentage of their sales that is imported or purchased from manufacturers other than their traditional suppliers. It will also send an annual questionnaire to foreign-owned flat glass suppliers doing business in Japan to assess their efforts. In addition, the government will promote increased competition in the procurement of glass for both private and public-sector construction projects. Finally, the energy conservation standards for housing will be amended in a manner that promotes the use of insulating and safety glass, an area where foreign producers are very competitive. The US Government will also take measures in this area.[70]

Autos and auto parts

The most contentious area of the framework talks were the long consultations on autos and auto parts, which focused on the question of dealerships and the deregulation of the market for replacement auto parts.[71] These issues were substantially resolved in June 1995, outside the framework talks, when five Japanese car manufacturers announced plans to increase their production in foreign countries and to purchase more foreign auto parts. The US Government expects that these plans will boost Japanese car production in North America. Both the Japanese and US authorities recognised, however, that such plans are not commitments subject to the trade remedy laws of either country and that their realisation may be affected by changing market conditions. Given the sharp rise of the yen against the dollar in early 1995, Japanese car manufacturers would probably increase their production in foreign countries even in the absence of the trade dispute between the two countries.

Although some concern has been expressed that Japanese firms may discriminate in favour of American auto parts, past efforts by the Japanese and US governments, including the 1987 measures, resulted in substantial export increases for non-US suppliers. Moreover, the Japanese firms avoided making projections of their future purchases of US auto parts as was done in 1991.[72] Meanwhile, US car manufacturers signalled their intention to increase their commercial presence in Japan, for example by investing in their own dealer networks and producing more right-hand-drive cars.

The Japanese Government's role is limited to the issues of auto dealerships and the auto inspection system. The government will welcome the development of a multi-brand dealership system by affirming the freedom of all dealers to sell foreign cars.[73] In addition, it will conduct a survey to determine how many domestic dealers are willing to sell foreign cars. It also announced its intention to partially deregulate the auto inspection system by easing the requirements for the establishment of "designated garages", the only service facilities allowed to conduct the vehicle inspections *(shaken)* required by law and to make the necessary repairs.[74]

Inward direct investment and buyer-supplier relationships

In July 1995, Japan announced measures to promote inward direct investment by removing unnecessary regulations and by implementing policies to reduce the start-up costs for new foreign investors. For example, the Japan Development Bank will continue to make low-interest loans available to foreign firms wishing to invest in Japan. The government will also extend the Inward Investment Law, which provides tax incentives and loan guarantees to foreign firms. In addition, foreign investors can now carry forward business losses for up to ten years, rather than the previous seven-year limit, to help them cope with the high initial cost of investing in Japan. These measures will be co-ordinated by the Japan Investment Council, an advisory body established in July 1994 and headed by the prime minister. Furthermore, the government will take steps to facilitate mergers and acquisitions involving foreign firms by strengthening shareholders' rights and preventing restrictive business practices. Finally, Japan and the United States confirmed their support for negotiations within the OECD to create a "Multilateral Agreement on Investment".

Global assessment

The deregulation process in Japan has become significantly more transparent. The annual review of the March 1995 package, drawing on the ideas of interested parties both domestic and foreign, should help promote effective reform. The implementation of the Administrative Procedures Law, which is intended to clarify government procedures, should contribute to ensuring that the benefits of deregulation are not offset by increased administrative guidance. In addition, the strengthened enforcement of competition policy may help to prevent restrictive business practices.

Despite the slow pace of deregulation overall, there have been profound changes in some sectors, such as distribution. However, it appears unlikely that the latest government package will substantially accelerate the process. Indeed, many of the measures included in the new plan are aimed at the same sectors as previous deregulation plans, suggesting a degree of repetition and overlap and a continuation of a strategy based on incremental change. In addition, some of the measures simply commit the government to review certain regulations, with no indication as to whether this will lead to an abolition or simply an easing of regulations.[75] The new package's guideline concerning economic regulations – freedom in principle and regulation as the exception – suggests that the goal should be to eliminate, rather than merely relax, such regulations. Nonetheless, the fact that more than one-quarter of the proposals submitted by the private

Table 20.   **Number of regulations and permits by agency or ministry**

	1990	1993	1994			Change between 1994 and	
			Regulations added	Regulations removed	New Total	1990	1993
MITI	1 908	1 986	106	323	1 769	−139	−217
Ministry of Transport	1 988	1 893	61	254	1 700	−288	−193
MAFF	1 299	1 427	44	52	1 419	120	−8
Ministry of Finance	1 195	1 387	38	34	1 391	196	4
Ministry of Health and Welfare	1 033	1 221	31	6	1 246	213	25
Ministry of Construction	808	910	19	50	879	71	−31
Ministry of Labour	559	631	39	41	629	70	−2
Ministry of Education	315	333	1	7	327	12	−6
Science and Techonology Agency	291	303	0	2	301	10	−2
Ministry of Posts and Telecommunications	306	319	4	32	291	−15	−28
Environment Agency	162	188	7	1	194	32	6
Ministry of Justice	153	172	1	1	172	19	0
National Security Agency	100	134	15	5	144	44	10
Ministry of Home Affairs	113	134	2	9	127	14	−7
National Land Agency	86	89	0	1	88	2	−1
Ministry of Foreign Affairs	46	53	1	4	50	4	−3
MCA	34	37	0	2	35	1	−2
Prime Minister's Office	32	33	0	1	32	0	−1
Okinawa Development Agency	32	32	1	1	32	0	0
Hokkaido Development Agency	31	32	0	1	31	0	−1
Defence Agency	31	31	1	1	31	0	0
Economic Planning Agency	31	31	1	1	31	0	0
Fair Trade Commission	28	26	0	0	26	−2	0
Total	10 581	11 402	372	829	10 945	364	−457

Source: Management and Coordination Agency.

sector and foreign governments were rejected suggests the difficulty of implementing difficult reforms. As in most countries, this may reflect the power of existing vested interests in the private sector and some reluctance on the part of ministries to reduce their own power by eliminating or relaxing the regulations they enforce. Hence, the establishment of a powerful, independent organisation, as proposed in the 1993 Hiraiwa Report, may be a more effective way of promoting deregulation. The Administrative Reform Committee, which was created in December 1994, is supposed to function as such an organisation.

A thorough review of all existing regulations during the next five years would also be beneficial, since their number is still high despite the emphasis on deregulation in recent years (Table 20). Many regulations, which were intended to promote the economic and social development of Japan, should be reviewed in light of changing conditions.[76] A review process should lead to the elimination of those regulations that are not explicitly linked to basic policy objectives. Requiring the JFTC to review all new proposed regulations would help ensure that regulatory changes are consistent with competition policy. In addition, the government could estimate the enforcement and compliance costs of proposed regulations to determine whether the benefits justify the costs. Finally, every new regulation should be subject to mandatory review after a limited period.

IV. The transformation of the distribution system

The emergence of falling prices in Japan since mid-1994 has focused attention on the so-called "retail revolution" which has resulted in increased competition and has reduced costs in the domestic distribution sector. In part, this revolution, led by discount stores, reflects the weak economic environment which has led a growing number of shops to reduce their prices in response to stagnating sales and increasing retail capacity. But these developments are also due to the rise in the number of larger, more efficient stores which has been made possible by the relaxation of legal entry barriers.

By amplifying the decline in prices, which has its origin primarily in the growing gap between supply and demand brought about by slow growth, the reduction in distribution costs has boosted consumers' real incomes. Nonetheless, the price level in Japan remains high by international standards. Other parts of the service sector, in particular, are highly regulated and suffer from low productivity. In many areas, further deregulation and greater openness to international competition could raise incomes in Japan and broaden the progress achieved in the distribution sector.

The present chapter attempts to shed light on these issues by examining the main features of the Japanese distribution sector, its recent evolution following partial deregulation and the implications for price-setting behaviour. It then discusses further policy changes to build on recent developments and so ensure that there is a continued reduction in the price level in Japan relative to other countries.

Main features of the system

Structure

Japan has a large number of retail stores with low labour productivity. Relative to the population, the number of stores was more than double that in the United States, Germany or the United Kingdom in the mid-1980s (Table 21). Moreover, given the high population density in Japan, there were 20 times more stores per square kilometre than in the United States and three times as many as in the major countries of western Europe. Despite the large number of stores, the share of the distribution sector in the total output of the economy[77] and employment was slightly below the OECD average in 1990 (Table 22).[78] The value added per worker in the Japanese distribution system was 12 per cent below the OECD average when measured at market exchange rates and excluding the impact of indirect taxes. However, when measured at purchasing power parity

Table 21. **International comparison of store density**

	Japan 1985	United States 1982	Germany 1985	France 1987	United Kingdom 1984
Retail					
All retail stores					
Number of stores (1 000)	1 629.0	1 731.0	. .	565.0	343.0
Stores per 1 000 persons	13.4	7.5	6.7	10.3	6.1
Stores per 100 sq km	431.0	18.0	164.0	100.0	100.0
Workers per shop	3.9	7.5	5.8	3.9	6.8
Food stores					
Number of stores	671.0	165.0	. .	191.0	107.0
Stores per 1 000 persons	5.5	0.7	. .	3.5	1.9
Stores per 100 sq km	178.0	1.7	. .	34.0	44.0
Non-food stores					
Number of stores	957.0	1 566.0	. .	374.0	136.0
Stores per 1 000 persons	7.9	6.8	. .	6.8	4.2
Stores per 100 sq km	253.0	16.3	. .	66.0	56.0
Wholesale stores					
Stores per 1 000 persons	3.4	1.6	2.1	2.9	. .
Stores per 100 sq km	109.3	4.0	50.5	29.0	. .
Workers per shop	9.7	12.6	7.0	9.9	. .
Workers per 100 retailers	85.0	196.0	309.0	28.5	. .
Wholesale/retail sales	4.2	1.9	1.8	1.6	. .

Source: Kakeda (1994), "Changes in Japan's Distribution Structure", in *Japanese Distribution Channels*, edited by T. Kikuda.

Table 22. **The importance of the distribution sector in the economy**

1990

Countries ranked by increasing level of productivity

	Share in economy Per cent		Productivity market exchange rates $ 1 000		Productivity PPP exchange rates $ 1 000	
	Employment	Net output	Gross output per person employed	Net output per person employed	Gross output per person employed	Net output per person employed
Portugal	16.1	16.1	25.9	19.3	28.7	21.4
Finland	18.3	10.8	68.3	39.7	41.0	23.8
Canada	19.1	12.1	39.6	28.8	38.7	28.2
Spain	19.5	15.2	43.1	33.7	37.6	29.4
Sweden	17.8	10.2	57.1	39.4	42.6	29.4
Norway	19.4	11.0	57.9	42.4	40.5	29.6
Japan	**19.4**	**13.8**	**50.2**	**34.4**	**43.3**	**29.7**
Germany	16.3	9.8	n.a.	35.7	n.a.	31.5
Italy	21.0	16.7	n.a.	42.2	n.a.	35.8
Luxembourg	18.7	15.9	n.a.	40.2	n.a.	37.9
Denmark	15.9	12.6	69.4	50.2	53.1	38.3
Netherlands	20.5	14.3	64.5	40.8	61.2	38.7
Iceland	15.4	13.5	64.4	57.0	43.9	38.9
Austria	18.4	15.2	62.2	46.1	54.0	40.0
France	18.9	14.3	63.3	51.6	52.5	42.9
United States	25.3	17.0	53.4	41.4	66.5	51.4
Average	21.3	14.8	52.5	39.2	55.8	40.8
(unweighted)	18.8	13.7	55.3	40.2	46.4	34.2

Source: OECD.

exchange rates, labour productivity was 25 per cent below the OECD average.[79] Only Portugal and Finland have significantly lower productivity.

The low level of labour productivity in the Japanese distribution sector is associated with the large number of small shops with only one or two workers. These account for 14 per cent of total retail sales, double the share of such shops in the United States and Germany[80] (Table 23). The size distribution of stores in Japan, though, is similar to that in France, reflecting the much higher number of food stores per person in these two countries. The number of other types of retail stores shows much less variation across countries, although Japan still has almost 20 per cent more non-food stores per person than the United States and France. Overall, in 1990 the number of stores per inhabitant in Japan was 27 per cent

Table 23. **International comparison of store sizes**

1982

Workers per store Persons			Share of sales Per cent				Sales per worker $ thousand		
Japan[1]	US[2]	France	**Japan**	US	France	Germany[3]	**Japan**	US	France
1-2		0-2	**14.0**	6.9	18.9	6.6	**33**	99	56
3-4		3-5	**18.9**	7.5	19.6	21.8	**54**	96	58
5-9		6-9	**22.0**	16.2	13.3	..	**75**	86	65
	10-19		**12.5**	14.8	10.7	10.6	**70**	86	79
	20-49		**12.6**	21.4	12.7	10.9	**71**	112	100
	50-99		**5.8**	16.6	6.0	5.8	**77**	122	96
	>100		**14.3**	16.6	18.8	44.2	**128**	81	102
Small scale			**32.9**	14.4	38.5	..	..	..	..
Large scale			**20.1**	13.2	24.8	..	..	..	..

1. Includes the owner as a worker.
2. Excludes the owner.
3. By enterprise.
Source: Nishimura (1995), "Entry Regulations, Tax Distortions and the Bipolarized Market: The Japanese Retail Sector", Discussion Paper 94-F-23, *Research Institute for the Japanese Economy.*

higher than in the weighted average for the remainder of the OECD area, while the number of employees was 22 per cent lower (Table 22).

The Japanese distribution system is also characterised by a large number of wholesalers compared with the United States and Germany (Table 21). On the other hand, Japan has nearly as many wholesalers relative to population as France. The similarity with France suggests that the large size of the wholesale sector in Japan is linked to the small size of stores in the retail sector. The wholesale system is also distinguished by a large number of layers, as shown by the high ratio of wholesale to retail turnover which reflects the importance of transactions between wholesale firms. The large number of wholesalers relative to retailers does not necessarily indicate inefficiency. Instead, it may be linked to the extremely high stock turnover (ratio of sales to stocks) in Japanese retail stores and the consequent need for frequent and relatively small deliveries. A comparison of a leading Japanese retail company with an American one shows that, for a similar size of store, the stock turnover is almost five times greater in Japan. This is due to the lower amount of inventory held in the shop and much higher sales per square metre (Table 24). Such intensive use of space stems from high land prices, which push capital costs per square metre to five times the level

Table 24. **A comparison between a US and a Japanese large-scale retailer**

		US retailer[1]			Japanese retailer[1]		
		1990	1991	1992	1990	1991	1992
Store number		1 549	1 759	1 900	119	118	119
Store size	sq metres	7 442	7 954	8 832	8 881	9 079	9 482
Sales per sq metre	¥ 000	311	345	364	1 172	1 234	1 213
Investment per sq metre	¥ 000	77	87	102	270	293	302
Capital	¥ 000	47	56	66	294	326	333
Stocks	¥ 000	30	31	35	−25	−33	−31
Gross margin	per cent	22	20.9	20.5	28.4	27.8	27.6
Costs	per cent	13.9	13.2	13	20.9	19.6	19.5
Profit margin	per cent	8.1	7.7	7.5	7.5	8.2	8.1
Rate of return	per cent	35	33	30	33	35	33

1. The two companies are Wallmart for the US and the superstore subsidiary of Ito-Yokado.
Source: Goldman Sachs and OECD calculations.

seen in the United States. High storage costs make it efficient to have a large number of wholesalers. Part of the high capital cost is met by the wholesaler and manufacturer, who finance the retailer's inventory.

Although Japanese stores tend to be relatively small, there are about 2 500 large stores with an average size of about 8 000 square metres. While this category only has 0.2 per cent of all stores in Japan, it accounts for about 20 per cent of sales (Figure 36). In contrast, small shops, with an average size of 12 square metres, account for nearly a quarter of all stores, but only 5 per cent of sales. The number of these small shops, which was constant at around one million until the beginning of the 1980s, has since fallen by about 30 per cent.

Labour productivity in Japanese stores rises markedly as the size of a shop increases (Figure 37, Panel A). Sales per employee in the largest stores are about six times higher than in the smallest shops. For food stores, the economies of scale for labour appear to be fully exploited at a size of around 1 000 square metres. Moreover, sales per square metre begin to decline at that size. For non-food stores, though, economies of scale continue even at the largest store size while there is only slight evidence of diseconomies of scale in sales per square metre. Further scale economies could also be realised by the centralisation of management functions achieved through one company owning a chain of stores, or several chains of stores, aimed at different categories. More effective merchan-

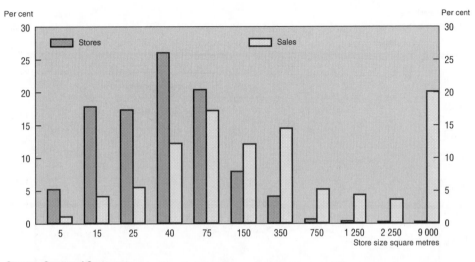

Figure 36. **DISTRIBUTION OF STORES AND SALES BY STORE SIZE**
1991

Source: Census of Commerce.

dising, logistics and purchasing could be expected from such regroupings. There was a trend toward larger stores in the 1970s as supermarket chains were first developed. The market share of retail enterprises employing more than 1 000 employees doubled from 9 per cent in 1970 to almost 18 per cent in 1980 and increased further to 21 per cent by 1990. Even so, the number of employees per store remains low in Japan and a significant part of the low productivity of the retail sector, relative to other countries, appears to be associated with the low average store size stemming from the large number of stores (Figure 37, Panel B).

Another distinguishing feature of the Japanese distribution sector is the extent of vertical integration. About 30 per cent of all wholesalers are affiliated with a *keiretsu*, a grouping of companies with long-term formal or informal linkages (Table 25). Whether the integration is horizontal or vertical depends on the type of wholesaler. The large ''first-level'' wholesalers are most likely to be vertically integrated with manufacturers. Second and third-level wholesalers are more likely to be grouped horizontally with other ones. The close links between manufacturers and wholesalers date back to the early 1900s when the latter

Figure 37. **PRODUCTIVITY AND STORE SIZE**
1991

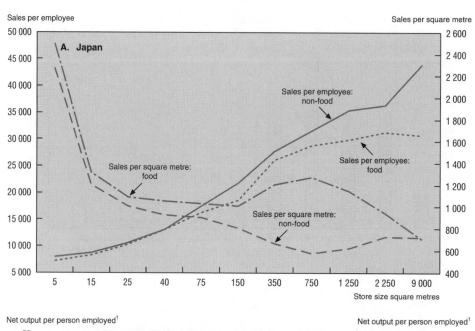

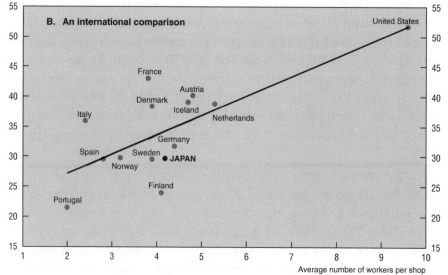

1. Thousands US$, converted at purchasing power parities.
Source: Survey of Commerce and OECD.

Table 25.   **The extent of vertical and horizontal integration**

1991

	Retailer integrated Per cent of enterprises			Extent of integration Per cent of sales
	Vertically	Horizontally	Total	Total
Retailers				
Furniture	10.0	7.3	17.3	22.2
Clothing	11.0	6.0	17.0	21.5
Food	11.8	10.7	22.5	30.7
General merchandise	16.3	9.3	25.6	26.4
Other retailing	16.9	9.4	26.3	36.6
Cars	32.5	11.2	43.7	55.4
Pharmaceutical	40.1	0.8	40.9	34.3
Fuel distribution	63.9	7.2	71.1	80.4
Appliances	67.9	6.5	74.4	66.1
All retail	19.8	9.1	28.9	39.3
	Wholesaler integrated Per cent of enterprises			Extent of integration Per cent of sales
	Vertically	Horizontally	Total	Total
Wholesalers				
First level wholesalers	19.6	11.4	31.0	36.5
Second level wholesalers	11.4	20.6	32.0	33.7
Third level wholesalers	11.3	18.4	29.7	32.2
All wholesalers	15.8	14.9	30.7	34.7

Source: Ministry of International Trade and Industry, *Basic Survey of Commercial Structure and Activity.*

financed and controlled the former. Today ownership or control of wholesalers by manufacturers is more typical. The extent of vertical integration is greater amongst retailers than wholesalers, especially for the distribution of durables where it is the predominant retail structure. Even without formal membership in a *keiretsu*, Japanese business practices, which favour continuity in transactions and discourage dealing with newcomers, tend to link wholesalers and manufacturers. Many business practices, such as open-ended returns and rebates, were introduced by manufacturers to develop networks with retailers and thus help promote mass marketing. These practices have enabled Japan to achieve results similar to those accomplished elsewhere through vertical integration of the manufacturer/ wholesale/retail chain while keeping a fragmented retail system. Their primary purpose appears to be to improve information flows and hence reduce risk. This wholesale structure may raise distribution costs as retailers have to deal with many wholesalers. In contrast, a wholesaler handles a wide range of products in the United States.

Driving forces

Economic factors favour a dense shopping network in Japan. Consumers' preferences for service, freshness and quality help determine the size and density of the distribution system. The costs of shopping trips and storage also enter into consumers' decisions on how often to shop and how far to travel. Differences in these preferences and costs across countries mean that a distribution network that is optimal in one country may not be so in another. Consequently, two distribution systems that differ in productivity levels can still be economically efficient in their own environment. In the case of Japan, the high number of stores, and hence low productivity, reflects the relatively high storage costs for consumers due to the high price of land. Wholesalers are able to locate in less expensive areas and develop efficient storage systems. They are also able to deliver to the shops more easily than consumers can drive to stores – at least in metropolitan areas.

Government regulation is another reason for the persistence of a fragmented retail system in Japan. The most important regulation is the Large-Scale Retail Store (LSRS) law, which was enacted in 1974 to replace an earlier law governing the establishment of department stores. The LSRS law controlled both the establishment of new stores with a surface area of more than 1 500 square metres and the expansion of existing stores beyond that size limit. It required a prospective store owner to notify the government of plans to open a store. The proposal was first examined by the "Committee to Adjust Commercial Activities" (CACA), which was established by the local Chamber of Commerce. This committee reported its findings to LSRS Council which, in turn, issued a report to the government on the desirability of opening a large store. However, the law only gave the government power to delay proposals by a maximum of six months. Consequently, the number of large store notifications under the law increased to an average of 300 per year between 1974 and 1979. In addition, the LSRS law regulated the number of days that a store must close each year and its opening hours.

A new LSRS law, enacted in 1979, reduced the limit of application to 500 square metres and changed the procedures for opening a new store. Through administrative guidance in 1982, MITI also added a new preliminary stage to the procedure under which a potential retailer first had to negotiate an agreement with a group of local retailers, consumers and academics. The local governor could not accept a notification until such an approval had been granted. In practice, this gave the existing retailers the ability to block all new development since there was no time limit on how long preliminary negotiations could take. In addition, the requirement for prior agreement created a new negotiable right for local store owners, who were able to demand benefits from a developer, such as favourable rents or good locations in the proposed store, in return for agreeing to the development.[81] Once the preliminary approval was obtained, the notification was officially filed for consideration by the CACA and the LSRS Council, which still only had the power to enforce a six-month delay. The CACA and the LSRS Council, in turn, made a recommendation either to the local prefectoral government or to the Minister of International Trade and Industry in the case of stores larger than 1 500 square metres (3 000 square metres in metropolitan areas).

The 1979 law, which was intended to decentralise the procedures for opening new stores, resulted in a wide range of new local laws. Many local governments enforced additional regulations or extended the application of the LSRS law to shops below 500 square metres. As a result, the number of applications to open new large stores fell substantially after 1979 (Figure 38).

Figure 38.   **APPLICATIONS FOR NEW LARGE SCALE STORES**[1]
Fiscal years

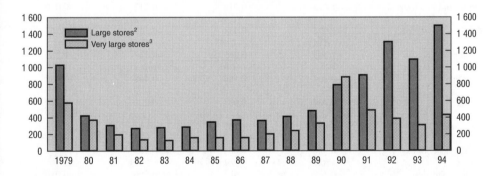

1.   The data shows the number of applications to open large stores under the provisions of Article 3 of the large scale stores law.
2.   A large store has a sales area between 500 and 3 000 square metres (500 and 1 500 sq metres prior to 1992).
3.   A very large store has a sales area of over 3 000 square metres (1 500 sq metres prior to 1992).
Source: MITI.

The impact of the LSRS law has been examined by two studies.[82] Both attempted to explain the variation in store density and size across prefectures using various economic factors, as well as regional differences in the implementation of the LSRS law.[83] One of the studies found that a 1 per cent increase in the number of department stores was associated with a 0.2 per cent fall in the total number of stores. Given that there are 500 ordinary stores for every department store, preventing the opening of one department store would appear to protect 100 ordinary stores from closure. The impact of the LSRS law appears to be greatest in the clothing and liquor sectors, while it is least for gasoline stations and car sales outlets as department stores do not compete in these areas (Table 26). According to this study, the location of department stores appears to

Table 26. **The determinants of retail store density in Japan**[1]

Variables which explain store density per household across Japanese local authority areas, multiple regression coefficients

Dependent variable Type of store Natural log	Independent variables			
	Population in dense areas Per cent of population	Living space Tatami mats	Motor vehicles per household Cars	Department store density Per household
All retailing	**−0.466**	0.005	**−0.166**	**−0.126**
	(−3.2)	*(0.3)*	*(−3.1)*	*(−2.3)*
Drugs and toiletries	**−1.415**	0.016	0.012	−0.016
	(−9.5)	*(0.9)*	*(0.2)*	*(−0.3)*
Food and beverages	**−1.994**	−0.038	**−0.523**	**−0.162**
	(−10.4)	*(−1.6)*	*(−7.4)*	*(−2.3)*
Liquor	**−1.363**	−0.045	**−0.824**	**−0.183**
	(−5.7)	*(−1.6)*	*(−9.4)*	*(−2.1)*
Gasoline	**−0.404**	**0.100**	**0.468**	−0.037
	(−2.4)	*(4.8)*	*(7.5)*	*(−0.6)*
Apparel	**−0.404**	**0.094**	0.221	**−0.184**
	(−2.3)	*(4.5)*	*(1.0)*	*(−2.9)*
Furniture	**−0.59**	**0.09**	0.21	−0.073
	(−4.1)	*(5.0)*	*(1.2)*	*(−1.4)*
Department stores	0.036	0.004	0.231	..
	(0.1)	*(0.1)*	*(0.4)*	..
Motor vehicles	**−0.562**	**0.1**	**0.996**	−0.016
	(−3.8)	*(5.6)*	*(5.5)*	*(−0.3)*
Hardware	**−1.198**	**0.061**	−0.042	−0.067
	(−7.9)	*(3.2)*	*(−0.2)*	*(−1.2)*

1. Figures in bold indicate that an independent variable is significant at the 5 per cent level. The t statistics are shown in italics and parenthesis.
Source: Flath, D., *Japan and the World Economy,* 1990, p. 365.

be determined less by economic criteria than by other factors, while economic influences are more important for other types of stores.

The same study also confirmed that high transport costs have helped preserve a fragmented distribution system. It found that regions with high levels of car ownership, and hence lower transport costs, have fewer stores. In addition, areas with high population density, which reduced the distance to stores, also had a lower store density. The second study, which used a more sophisticated measure of regulation based on a city-by-city study of regulations, suggested that large-scale stores of over 1 500 square metres gained a monopoly rent from regulation, which increased the level of sales per store.[84] High land prices increased small store density, perhaps since the inheritance tax encouraged small shopkeepers to retain their property.[85]

Overall, these studies suggest that while the LSRS law has had a significant impact on the number of stores during the 1980s, the main explanation lies in economic factors. In particular, high storage costs for families, stemming from high land prices, lead to frequent purchases of food and liquor, thus raising shopping costs. Consumers are prepared to pay higher prices in order to enjoy the benefits of shopping more frequently closer to home. However, as the population becomes more suburbanised and car ownership rises, household shopping costs and shop density may fall and the average shop size may increase. Indeed, the importance of economic factors in determining average store size has been confirmed by an analysis undertaken by the Secretariat.[86] This study found that factors specific to Japan, not all of which can be attributed to regulation, raised store density in Japan by only 10 per cent above that which would be expected on the basis of economic factors.[87]

Recent evolution of the system

The move towards deregulation

In the early 1990s, there were two reforms of the 1979 LSRS law. The *first*, in May 1990, cut the time between the filing of an initial request with the local government and the issuance of a ministerial recommendation to eighteen months; it also streamlined and relaxed the enforcement of certain provisions of the law. The *second* was the enactment of an amended LSRS law in January 1992 which made two major changes. An overall limit of one year was placed on the time for dealing with an application (Figure 39). In addition, the requirement to obtain preliminary approval was lifted and the CACAs were abolished. As a result, the applicant no longer has to negotiate directly with existing retailers and the prefectoral governor, an elected official, cannot refuse to accept a notification. The procedure was shortened to only one step – a strengthened hearings process in front of the LSRS Council. The Council does not include existing retailers and cannot delay a decision beyond the one-year time limit.

The amended LSRS law also provided for the supremacy of national over local laws. All local regulations and ordinances concerning stores of over

Figure 39. **THE NEW PROCEDURE FOR OPENING A LARGE STORE**

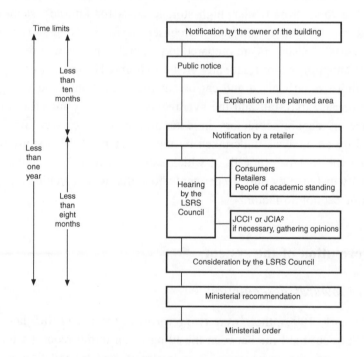

1. JCCI: the Japan Chamber of Commerce and Industry.
2. JCIA: the Japan Commerce and Industry Association.
Source: MITI.

500 square metres must now conform to the national law, thus prohibiting stricter controls by local authorities. On the other hand, more control over the implementation of the law was transferred to local authorities. All store notifications of less than 3 000 square metres (less than 6 000 square metres in metropolitan areas) are now decided by the prefectoral governor. Applications for larger stores are dealt with by the Minister of International Trade and Industry.[88] Stores of less than 1 000 square metres selling exclusively imported products were exempted from the LSRS law.

In May 1994, there was a third reform of the LSRS law, achieved by an easing of administrative procedures under the amended law. A potential retailer is now allowed to apply for development and construction permits at the same time that the notification under the LSRS law is filed, thus shortening the overall time required to establish a new store. The regulations regarding opening times were also relaxed. Large stores can now operate freely 341 days of the year and need permission to open only on the remaining 24 days – down from 44 days in 1990 and 48 days in 1973. In addition, stores were permitted to stay open until 8 p.m. (up from 7 p.m. in 1990 and 6 p.m. in 1973) and one hour later 60 days per year.

Legislation promoting the development of new shopping centres was also introduced in 1992. It authorised financial support, through loans from FILP institutions, for the creation of shopping centres with one or two large stores surrounded by a number of small ones. A joint body co-ordinating the views of MITI, the Ministry of Construction and the Ministry of Home Affairs was established for this purpose.

Retail distribution is restricted by a number of other regulations that relate primarily to safety and consumer protection. Some, however, also restrain entry in certain fields such as liquor retailing. The regulations governing this area, though, have been relaxed recently to allow stores of 10 000 square metres and over (less than 2 000 stores in the country) to freely obtain a liquor licence, although they cannot sell domestic beer and sake for a three-year period. However, the same regulations reinforced the prohibition on the purchase and sale of existing liquor licences, thus closing a loophole which had been an entry route for smaller newcomers. Nevertheless, the number of liquor licences has increased sharply since 1989.

Changes in the retailing framework

As a result of the liberalisation of the LSRS law, the number of new stores of over 500 square metres is increasing almost 12 per cent a year. The revision of the law has generated a significant rise in the number of applications to open large stores of between 500 and 3 000 square metres[89] (Figure 38). By fiscal year 1994, their number had increased sixfold from the low point seen in 1982 after the introduction of the 1979 law. Applications to open very large stores (over 6 000 square metres in Tokyo and other metropolitan areas and over 3 000 square metres elsewhere) rose by a factor of three. Moreover, a significant number of these new stores have more than 10 000 square metres. The new shopping centre law may also have boosted the creation of large stores by allowing supermarket companies to develop shopping centres with the supermarket as the anchor store.

The growing number of large stores has had a marked impact on the structure of the retail industry in the period 1991 to 1994. According to preliminary estimates, the total number of stores fell by 6½ per cent, the largest three-year decline since the Survey of Commerce started in the 1950s (Table 27).

Table 27. **Retail stores**

Per cent change 1991 to 1994

	Number of stores					Surface area	
		By business structure and size					
	All stores	Incorporated			Unincorporated		
		All firms	Small firms	Large firms	All	Average	Total
Department stores	8.2	10.0	3.8	14.4	1.8	7.1	15.9
Food	−8.5	0.9	−0.7	30.7	−12.0	13.0	3.4
Supermarkets	−5.2	0.2	−5.1	22.3	−9.2	8.8	3.1
Liquor	−13.3	−5.9	−6.1	25.3	−15.5	8.0	−6.4
Specialised food	−14.3	−3.3	−3.8	42.0	−17.6	30.9	12.1
Other	3.7	10.4	9.9	42.1	0.7	5.4	9.3
Clothing, textiles, shoes	−6.3	0.2	0.2	2.3	−11.1	13.7	6.5
Clothing (non-japanese)	−3.1	1.9	1.9	1.7	−7.4	14.4	10.8
Other	−10.1	−2.3	−2.3	2.9	−14.8	11.9	0.6
Furniture and other durables	−10.6	−5.4	−5.9	17.0	−13.6	16.1	3.8
Leisure and health	−3.4	5.4	4.7	26.4	−9.3	26.3	21.9
Motor vehicles	−4.2	1.7	1.8	−0.5	−9.6	73.1	65.8
Total	−6.6	1.8	1.0	22.5	−11.2	18.5	10.7

Source: Ministry of International Trade and Industry, *Preliminary Report of Census of Commerce.*

Although information on the size distribution of shops in 1994 has not yet been published, small stores appear to account for the bulk of store closures. The number of stores belonging to unincorporated businesses – the business structure used by small store owners – declined most rapidly while those owned by incorporated businesses rose by 2 per cent. Moreover, the Survey reported that the number of stores employing more than 20 persons rose by 22 per cent between 1991 and 1994. A further indication of an increase in the proportion of large stores is that the average store size rose by nearly 18 per cent between 1991 and 1994 – the same increase as recorded during the previous six years. As a result, total selling area expanded despite a fall in the number of stores. The rise in the number of large stores was particularly marked amongst general merchandise stores, supermarkets and liquor stores.

There has also been a marked increase in sales at discount stores since 1992, while those at traditional retailers, such as department stores and supermarkets, have been stagnant (Table 28). Discount stores' sales rose at an annual rate of 10 per cent in nominal terms, with growth concentrated in the food area. In the non-food sector, the market share of discounters rose from 4.2 per cent in 1988 to 5.6 per cent in 1993, reflecting rapid growth in sales of men's clothes and electronics.

The change in market structure is most striking in the area of men's clothing. Until 1991, this sector was dominated by department stores and large supermarkets, which together held over 40 per cent of the market. Between 1991 and 1993, though, department stores' sales of these items fell by 15 per cent while men's discount clothing stores saw their sales rise by 28 per cent. The change in market share was accompanied by a sharp fall in prices. The growth of discount stores has been aided by the weak retail management skills of the department stores, which benefited from the protection of the LSRS law and its predecessor, the Department Store Law. These stores rely heavily on wholesalers and manufacturers for inventory management, merchandising and sales promotion. Moreover, unsold goods can be returned to the wholesaler who thus carries the inventory risk for the department store. The wholesalers and manufacturers also supply sales staff to the department store. These, who account for as much as two-thirds of department stores' sales workers, are paid by the wholesaler. Such a system ties department stores into long-term, informal arrangements with their wholesalers and manufacturers, leaving little freedom to change suppliers.

Table 28. **Retail sales of discount stores**

	Sales Year ending March Billion yen						Average annual growth Per cent	
	1989	1990	1991	1992	1993	1994	1992/89	1994/92
Total	2 826	3 150	3 452	4 144	4 597	4 971	14	10
Market share	2.8			3.4		4.0		
Non-food discount stores	2 729	3 028	3 294	3 932	4 332	4 613	13	8
Market share	4.2			4.9		5.6		
General discount stores	981	1 073	1 109	1 111	1 133	1 184	4	3
Specialist discount stores	1 748	1 955	2 185	2 821	3 199	3 429	17	10
Home equipement	626	681	810	1 092	1 203	1 306	20	9
Men's clothes	204	239	300	368	440	471	22	13
Shoes	143	225	266	313	351	375	30	9
Drugs	136	112	143	214	249	248	16	8
Electronics	405	427	342	461	550	605	4	15
Sports goods	212	259	309	354	380	393	19	5
Others	22	13	15	18	24	30	–6	29
Food discount stores	96	122	158	211	269	359	30	31
Food	54	64	53	90	105	165	18	35
Meat	17	27	52	63	70	65	54	1
Liquor	24	31	52	58	93	130	34	50
Memorandum item:								
Department stores	9 552	10 516	11 456	12 085	11 930	11 263	8	–3
Large supermarkets	8 332	8 859	9 485	10 079	10 273	10 226	7	1

Source: Nikkei Ryutsu Shimbin, Research Institute of the Retail Industry and Distribution System.

Department stores have essentially become property-owners who rent space to other retailers.[90] Despite this practice of sub-contracting, the department stores continue to have a high gross operating margin.

The discount stores have adopted a different approach. *First*, they moved from the city centre locations favoured by the department stores to suburban roadside locations. This enabled them to profit from the increased rate of car ownership, which rose from under 60 per cent of Japanese households at the beginning of the 1980s to nearly 80 per cent in 1991. However, the loosening of regulations in the new LSRS law has not been crucial to their development, as the average size of a typical discount clothing store is slightly under 400 square metres. *Secondly*, the companies undertook their own product development and merchandising. Rather than sell brand-name clothing, discounters offer "own-label'' products with quality similar to that of branded goods but with lower prices. The discounters design the product on the basis of the experience of their own sales staff and then contract production either to small Japanese firms or, increasingly, to companies in South-East Asia. Since the manufacturer has neither sales nor wholesaling costs, the discounter pays less for merchandise (Figure 40). Moreover, the discounter is able to benefit from competition between different manufacturers since it is not tied to one supplier of a branded good. As a result, a discount-type operation in the clothing sector can reduce the ratio of the

Figure 40. **COST STRUCTURES OF NEW AND TRADITIONAL RETAILERS MEN'S SUITS**

Yen

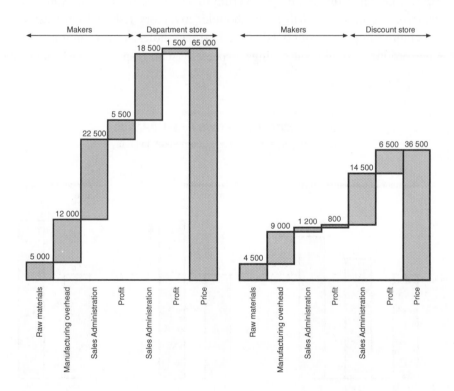

Source: The McKinsey Quarterly.

final product price to the raw material cost by half. This pattern has also spread to computers, electronics and more recently to liquor. However, the development of discount liquor stores is still restricted by licencing requirements, which play an important role in limiting the social consequences of alcohol.

The major supermarket chains are also changing their procurement patterns. In contrast to department stores, supermarket chains have been successful in controlling administrative and sales costs. As a result, increasing profits depends primarily on finding ways to reduce procurement costs, which account for 65 per cent of turnover. One way has been to increase own-label products purchased from smaller domestic manufacturers or imported. Although such sales have grown rapidly, they still accounted for only 1.5 per cent of a major supermarket chain's sales in 1993 (Figure 41). The main national brand producers have attempted to counter this trend by lowering their prices. In addition, supermarket chains have become more willing to shoulder inventory risk and purchase products, including imports, from outside the normal wholesale distribution network. This has produced significant savings, especially with respect to beef, juices and

Figure 41. **GROWTH OF OWN-LABEL BRANDS**

Sales in the largest japanese supermarket company

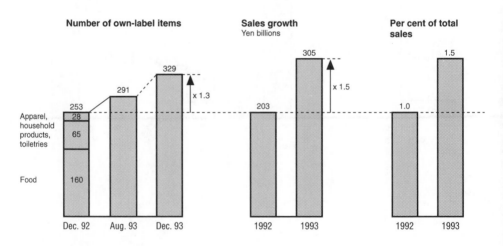

Source: Nikkan Suisan Keizai Shimbun.

dairy products where import barriers have been lowered. In part, the change in procurement patterns was made possible by the improved knowledge of market trends generated by advances in information technology. In some cases, this sales information has enabled manufacturers to collaborate directly with some supermarket chains and bypass traditional wholesale links. However, most national brand manufacturers remain wary of such direct links. But even if they do not deal directly with retailers, the fact that the supermarket chains are developing their own procurement channels is putting pressure on manufacturers to reduce the number of levels in the wholesale system.

Supermarket chains are more affected by the liberalisation of the LSRS law as the average size of a retail superstore is around 9 000 square metres. The change in the law is both a competitive threat to the superstores and an opportunity for their expansion. In addition, the new deflationary environment threatens the capital base of these retailers. As noted above, they usually take credit from suppliers due to favourable payment terms. With rising nominal turnover, this credit generates cash for the retailer. However, with falling prices and turnover, the amount of credit granted to retailers falls.

Consequences for price setting

A price "revolution"?

The structural changes outlined above have generated downward pressures on prices in the distribution sector. Indeed, the pricing strategies of the major retail chains in Japan appear to be changing. Historically, pricing was controlled by the manufacturer through the complex wholesale system. Manufacturers, who wished to minimise price differences between small and large stores, used to set prices to reflect the higher cost of servicing small stores. Larger stores, which had lower distribution costs, were not rewarded with lower prices but instead received volume rebates or limited-period special promotions. In contrast, the new retailing climate emphasises continuous low prices rather than temporary promotions. As a result, there is growing pressure on leading manufacturers to switch to an open pricing system which does not seek to standardise prices across stores.

There is considerable evidence that consumers have become more price sensitive and less willing to pay large premia for brand-name products. The switch to lower-priced goods is reflected in a sharp fall in a private sector unit value index, which declined by 6 per cent in the second half of 1994.[91] In contrast, the goods component of the CPI, which measures the prices of a fixed basket of goods, fell only slightly during the same period. Official statistics show a similar pattern. The gap between the unit value index and the CPI was largest for durable goods in 1993 and clothing in 1994 (Table 29). Such differences have occurred in the past, especially during recessions.

As is clear from the experience of the "discount" clothing stores, the increase in the quantity of imports since 1993 has put downward pressure on the domestic price level. Part of the rise in imports has been associated with the increased availability of low-priced Asian products. While these goods may be of lower quality, their price tends to reduce the premium which can be charged for higher quality products, thus pushing down the overall price level. In addition,

Table 29. **The CPI and unit values for durables and clothing**

Per cent increase compared with one year ago

		Durables		Clothing	
		Unit value Actual mix of products	CPI unit price Standard mix of products	Unit value Actual mix of products	CPI unit price Standard mix of products
1992	Q1	4.0	−2.0	0.8	4.1
	Q2	5.1	−2.0	0.5	3.8
	Q3	3.9	−1.8	−1.2	2.4
	Q4	3.6	−1.8	−1.2	1.4
1993	Q1	0.8	−1.7	−1.8	−0.4
	Q2	−6.2	−2.6	−4.2	−0.2
	Q3	−9.3	−3.7	−4.4	−0.5
	Q4	−9.9	−4.8	−5.5	−1.1
1994	Q1	−10.8	−6.2	−6.8	−1.4
	Q2	−10.6	−7.0	−5.3	−1.6
	Q3	−6.4	−7.4	−5.0	−2.0
	Q4	−6.2	−7.8	−5.9	−1.7
1995	Q1	−6.9	−8.0	−2.5	−1.6
	Q2	−1.6	−7.5	−1.1	−0.9

Source: Management and Coordination Agency.

increased imports are likely to boost competition in the domestic market. Evidence of the impact of both of these effects can be seen in the 7 per cent decline in wholesale prices[92] between 1990 and 1994 in industries which experienced rising import penetration (Table 30). In contrast, there was no fall in prices in industries where import penetration was stable. In commodity-type industries, such as non-ferrous metals, there were also significant falls in prices, although import penetration did not increase. This reflects the high degree of substitution between domestic and imported products, which limits discrepancies between domestic and world prices.

The progressive restructuring has led to improved productivity and hence to falls in the cost of distribution. The relative GDP deflator in distribution, which had fallen about 1 per cent annually during the 1980s, declined by 2 per cent in both 1992 and 1993 (Figure 42). Given that distribution accounts for 14 per cent of gross value added, the faster decline in distribution costs appears to be lowering the overall price level by about 0.1 to 0.2 per cent annually. Although such gains are small in terms of the current and prospective level of deflation in Japan, they represent significant increases in productivity and real incomes. Some of these gains, though, reflect the shift of costs – such as transportation and storage costs – to consumers and thus do not imply an increase in real incomes. In the five-year period following the relaxation of the LSRS law, the real income gain to consumers may have been as large as $45 billion (3/4 per cent of GDP), a significant benefit from a structural policy change. Moreover, if the law were to be abolished, the benefit to consumers could be even larger. For example, eliminating half of the productivity difference between Japanese and average OECD retailers would boost GDP by 2 per cent, an annual gain of $120 billion for Japanese consumers.

The impact of the macroeconomic environment

Although the retail revolution has had the effect of lowering prices, the depressed economic conditions and appreciation of the currency have been the major factors contributing to price deflation. Over the past fifteen years, the level of spare capacity and the unemployment rate have been associated with the rate of inflation (Figure 43). In fact, the current rate of deflation and unemployment are similar to those seen in 1987. But the relationship between these two variables also depends on the impact of expectations on the price formation

Table 30. **Import penetration and the domestic price level**

	Imports as per cent of total supply					
	1990	1991	1992	1993	1994	1994 Q4
IMPORT PENETRATION						
Increasing						
Textiles	15.6	17.4	20.2	23.7	28.1	30.3
Precision machinery	21.1	22.4	24.2	32.8	36.9	36.5
Electrical machinery	4.9	5.1	5.8	7.3	9.0	9.7
Chemicals	9.6	10.0	8.1	10.8	11.9	13.2
Total of above	**8.3**	**8.7**	**9.2**	**11.4**	**13.1**	**14.2**
Stable						
Metal products	1.8	2.2	2.2	2.3	2.8	3.1
Transportation machinery	4.0	3.7	3.8	4.1	5.6	6.1
General machinery	4.0	4.2	4.6	4.7	5.4	5.7
Ceramics	3.1	3.0	2.9	2.9	3.3	3.5
Plastics	1.5	1.6	1.8	2.2	2.9	3.1
Processed food	6.2	5.5	5.2	4.9	5.1	5.1
Total of above	**3.5**	**3.4**	**3.5**	**3.7**	**4.6**	**4.9**
Commodity products						
Pulp	4.5	4.5	4.8	5.2	5.8	5.7
Petroleum derivatives	20.1	16.6	15.5	13.7	13.8	13.7
Iron and steel	3.8	4.5	3.6	4.1	3.9	4.3
Non-ferrous metals	21.7	21.6	18.7	19.3	20.0	21.2
Total of above	**10.9**	**10.5**	**9.6**	**9.6**	**9.9**	**10.2**
	Index 1990 = 100, domestic production for the domestic market					
DOMESTIC WHOLESALE PRICE						
Increasing import penetration						
Textiles	100	102.3	100.5	96.0	94.8	94.6
Precision machinery	100	100.5	101.0	101.2	99.6	99.2
Electrical machinery	100	96.9	94.9	92.7	90.2	88.7
Chemicals	100	103.0	98.7	95.8	93.5	93.9
Total of above	100	**99.4**	**97.0**	**94.4**	**92.1**	**91.4**
Stable penetration						
Metal products	100	102.1	101.9	100.3	98.6	98.3
Transportation machinery	100	99.8	100.5	100.2	99.2	98.6
General machinery	100	101.4	101.6	101.0	99.9	99.4
Ceramics	100	103.5	103.4	102.2	100.3	100.2
Plastics	100	106.4	103.9	100.7	98.0	97.6
Processed food	100	104.0	105.7	105.6	105.5	105.1
Total of above	100	**102.5**	**102.8**	**101.9**	**100.8**	**100.4**
Commodity products						
Pulp	100	102.9	101.8	101.0	99.0	99.3
Petroleum derivatives	100	102.3	96.3	91.8	87.2	87.9
Iron and steel	100	101.4	99.8	95.2	90.3	90.3
Non-ferrous metals	100	92.3	85.9	78.1	78.7	82.7
Total of above	100	**100.3**	**97.0**	**92.6**	**98.4**	**90.3**

Source: Bank of Japan and Ministry of Finance.

Figure 42. **DISTRIBUTION PRICES RELATIVE TO THE OVERALL PRICE LEVEL**

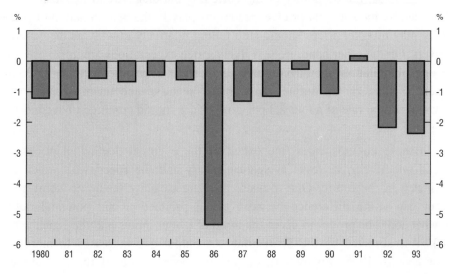

Source: National Accounts.

Figure 43. **CPI INFLATION AND THE UNEMPLOYMENT RATE**

Source: OECD.

process.[93] Thus, the durability of the current deflationary trend in Japan will be influenced by the role that price expectations play in the determination of prices. If they play no role, prices should stop falling relatively quickly as the economy recovers. On the other hand, if, as is likely, price expectations are important, then the rate of deflation should continue to increase even after activity picks up. Indeed, as long as the output gap remains negative and unemployment stays above its natural rate of about 2.3 per cent, prices should continue to decline at an increasing rate.

In these circumstances, the extent of the eventual decline in prices will depend on the current level of spare capacity and the speed with which it is eliminated in the future. One measure of spare capacity in the economy is the output gap – the difference between actual production and potential output, *i.e.* what could be produced given the trend of labour inputs and the actual capital stock. As estimated by the Secretariat, the output gap increased to more than 3 per cent in 1995 (Figure 44), despite the deceleration of the medium-term growth potential to as low as 2½ per cent.[94] Although the Japanese economy

Figure 44. **OUTPUT GAP AND THE UNEMPLOYMENT RATE**

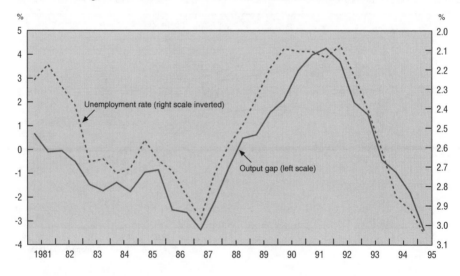

Source: OECD.

showed signs of recovery in late 1993, the output gap, which is closely linked to the unemployment rate has continued to widen. This correlation may suggest that a 1 per cent change in output is associated with a 0.15 percentage point change in the unemployment rate, indicating that the so-called "Okun's Law" (*i.e.* the inverse relationship between GDP and the unemployment rate) is valid in Japan, although with a much lower coefficient than in the United States, where a 1 point change in output is associated with a ⅓ point change in the unemployment rate.

Movements in the exchange rate have also had significant consequences for price setting. However, the direct impact of the yen's rise since 1993 on the price level has been small compared with the extent of the appreciation. Since imports account for only 8 per cent of total demand in Japan, the 30 per cent increase in the exchange rate between 1993 and 1995 by itself lowered the value of imports by about 2½ per cent of total demand. Once lower import costs have been passed through into final demand, the overall price level should fall by a similar amount. Part of the impact of the appreciation, though, has been offset by an increase in import prices. As a result, the yen appreciation reduced the price level by only 2 per cent in the period 1993-95 (Table 31). In contrast, the impact of the yen's rise in 1986 on the domestic price level was significantly amplified by the simultaneous fall in the price of oil.

The impact of exchange rate changes that occurred between 1993 and 1995 on the overall price level has been more spread out over time compared with the 1986 episode. The currency appreciation is reflected in the overall price level

Table 31. **Import prices and the overall price level** [1]

| | Change in effective exchange rate (appreciation negative) | | Change in import values relative to sales assuming | | | |
| | | | Constant import prices | | Actual import prices | |
	1993	1995	1993	1995	1993	1995
United States	−2.1	3.8	−0.3	0.5	−0.4	0.6
Japan	**−19.6**	**−12.8**	**−1.6**	**−1.0**	**−1.0**	**−1.0**
Germany	−2.0	−5.3	−0.5	−1.3	0.0	−0.5
France	−0.5	−1.3	0.0	−0.3	−0.5	0.2
Italy	16.0	15.5	3.4	3.7	2.2	2.8
United Kingdom	3.7	4.8	1.0	1.4	2.1	1.2
Canada	5.9	0.2	2.0	0.0	1.6	0.9

1. The table uses exchange rates of July 1995.
Source: OECD.

with a delay, since distributors and manufacturers initially increase their profit margins. The full pass-through of the appreciation to consumer prices takes about eighteen months, with an estimated 19 per cent in the first six months and a further 38 per cent in the following semester. Consequently, almost half of the pass-through occurs between twelve and eighteen months after the appreciation (Table 32). The combination of the appreciation occurring over a three-year period and the delays in passing it on have smoothed out the impact of the exchange rate on prices and may give the impression that the pass-through has speeded up.

A comparison of the movements of the GDP deflator and of the exchange rate shows the extent to which the delayed pass-through of the appreciation has indeed affected the price level (Figure 45). In the initial phase of the yen appreciation in 1993, the rate of increase of the GDP deflator moved above its trend rate as distributors gained windfall profits. When the exchange rate stabilised during 1994, the GDP deflator decelerated as the earlier appreciation was finally reflected in expenditure prices. While the short-term movements of

Table 32. **The link between import prices, wholesale prices and the CPI**
1985-1993

| | Independent variables | | | | | |
	Wholesale prices	Import prices	Output gap	Unit labour cost	R2	DW
Regression results&norm[1]						
Dependent variable						
Wholesale prices	–	0.122	0.425	0.442	0.96	1.04
	–	(7.3)	(4.0)	(7.4)	–	–
Consumer prices	0.209	0.142	–	0.553	0.99	1.26
	(1.6)	(3.1)	–	(2.8)	–	–

| | Impact of import prices on | | Impact of wholesale prices on consumer prices |
	wholesale prices	consumer prices	
Lag structure			
Current quarter	46.2	10.6	0.0
One quarter lag	33.3	20.6	0.0
Two quarters lag	20.4	30.0	0.0
Three quarters lag	0.0	39.3	0.0
Four quarters lag	0.0	0.0	18.9
Five quarters lag	0.0	0.0	43.7
Six quarters lag	0.0	0.0	37.4

1. The data sample is quarterly and the variables are measured as four quarter rates of changes.
Source: Economic Planning Agency.

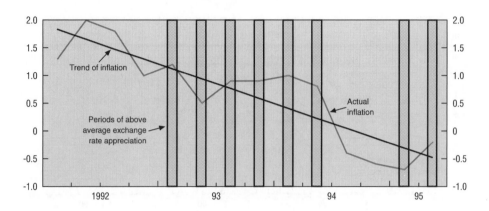

1. The trend of inflation has been determined by calculating a linear regression of the inflation rate on time between 1992 and 1995. The shaded histogram refer to periods when the exchange rate appreciated by more than the average amount seen over the past fifteen years.
    Source: OECD.

the GDP deflator in 1995 may have been influenced by the rise and subsequent fall of the yen, the continued high level of spare capacity may have continued to exert downward pressure on the price level. In contrast to the short-lived price decline in 1987, which was primarily due to the yen's sharp rise the previous year, this time the fall in the price deflator is expected to continue even after the pass-through of the 1995 yen appreciation is completed.

The current price level in an international perspective

Despite the recent deflation, Japan still has the highest overall price level in the OECD area. This reflects a long-term upward trend, which has boosted Japanese prices expressed in a common currency from 30 per cent below the OECD average in 1960 to 50 per cent above the average in 1993 (Figure 46). A similar, though less marked, movement occurred in Germany. In the United States, in contrast, the price level has declined relative to the OECD average.

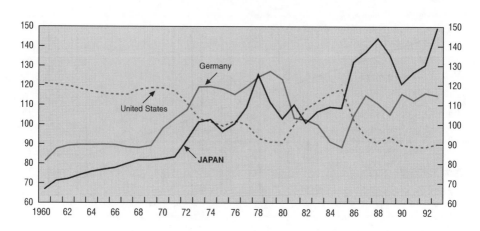

Figure 46. **RELATIVE PRICE LEVEL IN JAPAN AND SELECTED OTHER COUNTRIES**[1]

OECD = 100

1. The relative price for a country is measured as the ratio of purchasing power parity to the actual exchange rate.
    The price level for the OECD area is taken as 100 in each year.
Source: OECD, *National Accounts.*

There is generally a strong positive correlation between the level of income and the price level across OECD countries[95] (Figure 47). This is particularly the case for private and public services where international competition between countries with different income levels is relatively small. As a result, price levels tend to reflect cost (and hence income) levels (Panels C and D).[96] In contrast, the price of goods, where international competition is strongest, shows only a weak relationship with income levels (Panel B). In Portugal and Greece, for example, the price of goods was as high as the OECD average despite their lower-than-average income levels. Consequently, about three-quarters of the cross-country differences in incomes are reflected in price differentials (Panel A).[97]

Thus while the major part of the difference between prices in Japan and in other countries is accounted for by income levels in Japan, there nevertheless remains a substantial differential that cannot be explained in this way. The extent of this differential has fluctuated over time with movements in the exchange rate. Despite these movements, since the generalised floating of exchange rates in 1973, the price level in Japan has always been above that associated with the

110

Figure 47. **RELATIVE PRICE AND INCOME LEVELS**

1993, OECD = 100

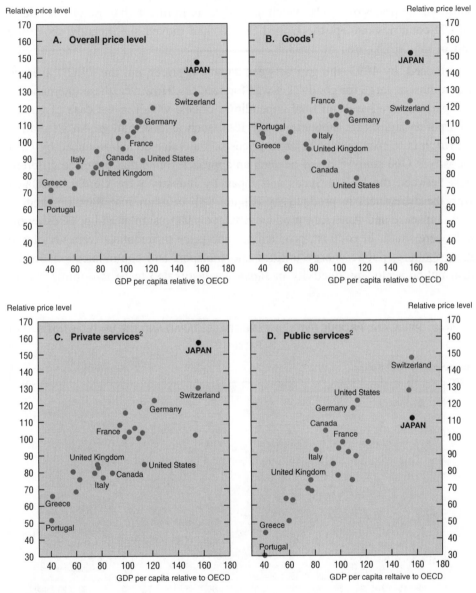

1. Excludes food.
2. Excludes private and public health care respectively.
Source: OECD.

income level. One reason is that private services appear somewhat overpriced relative to incomes, in contrast to the relatively low public service prices. In addition, the prices of goods, which in 1990 were in line with those of most other OECD countries (except the United States), had moved significantly above the rest of the OECD area by 1993.[98]

Indeed, by 1993, the gap between Japanese prices and the OECD average was almost as large for goods as it was for services. However, these international comparisons are based on final expenditure prices, which in the case of goods, incorporate significant amounts of services, such as distribution. An alternative approach is to measure the relative prices of the value-added produced by each industry.[99] One study[100] based on such an approach found that the price differentials between the United States and Japan by industry were closely correlated with the differences in productivity (Figure 48). In many manufacturing industries, Japanese and American productivity levels were similar and price differentials were small. In contrast, productivity and price differentials were very large in agriculture, public energy utilities and transport and communication. In the distribution sector, productivity in Japan was estimated to be two-thirds that in

Figure 48. **PRICE AND PRODUCTIVITY DIFFERENTIALS: JAPAN AND THE UNITED STATES, 1990**

Per cent

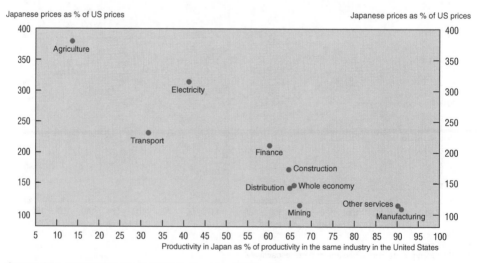

Source: Pilat, *Review of Income and Wealth,* December 1993, p. 35.

the United States, where the price of distribution services was almost 50 per cent lower.

Competition-restraining regulation may be one factor reducing Japanese productivity relative to the United States. One indicator of the extent of regulation is the percentage of value added that is affected by either pricing or entry barriers. These regulations are the lowest in manufacturing and real estate industries. In contrast, many industries, such as agriculture, finance, transportation and communications, mining, construction and energy production are almost entirely regulated (Table 33). These highly regulated sectors tend to have low productivity relative to the United States (Figure 48).

Table 33. **The extent of regulation by industry**[1, 2, 3]

1993

Item	Total value-added amount Trillion Yen	Share of total Per cent	Total amount of regulated areas Trillion Yen	Share of regulated areas in each industry Per cent
Industry				
Agriculture, forestry and fisheries	10.2	2.3	8.9	87.1
Mining	1.1	0.3	1.1	100.0
Construction	4.1	9.2	4.1	100.0
Manufacturing	115.4	25.9	16.2	14.1
Wholesaling and retailing	57.5	12.8	..	..
Finance, insurance and securities	22.0	4.9	22.0	100.0
Real estate	42.0	9.4	3.2	7.5
Transportation, communications	27.5	6.2	26.8	97.3
Electricity, gas, water and heat supply	10.8	2.4	10.8	100.0
Services, *of which:*				
Education, medical and welfare	101.7	22.8	56.5	55.6
Public services	14.5	3.2	0	0.0
Others	2.3	0.5	0	0.0
Total	446.1	100.0	183.4	41.8

1. In this table the existence of any type of related law for one of the industrial categories defined in the Input-Output Table is treated as applying to the entire industry. Therefore, it is necessary to note that even if deregulation occurs within a specific legal framework, the share of regulated areas does not change.
2. Even in cases where the related law only applies to a portion of the subject area, the entire added-value amount is counted as part of the regulated area value.
3. Within each area, those categories in the Input-Output Table for which it is difficult to ascertain whether a related law exists are not counted.
Source: Economic Planning Agency

International surveys of "factory gate" prices show a much smaller gap between Japan and other countries than the purchasing power parity studies using final sales prices. The latter indicated a 50 per cent price differential for goods between the United States and Japan in 1994 and a 35 per cent difference between Germany and Japan. According to surveys of factory-gate prices, the differentials with the United States and Germany were only 14 and 3 per cent, respectively (Figure 49). The differentials are lower because the wholesale price of goods incorporates less services. There were, however, considerable variations in the price differentials across services. The factory-gate surveys, for example, found large international price differentials for services and input products that are potentially tradable on an international basis. Services, such as international air freight, telephone calls and financial transactions, as well as energy products, were between 30 and 150 per cent higher than in the United States and Germany.

Figure 49. **FACTORY-GATE PRICE DIFFERENTIALS BETWEEN JAPAN, THE UNITED STATES AND GERMANY**[1]

April-September 1994

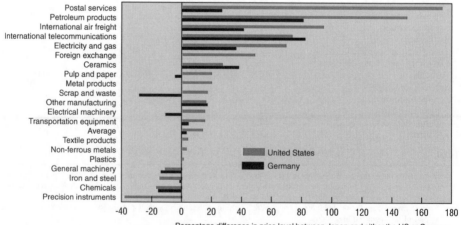

1.   The prices are those paid or received by manufactures.
Source: MITI, *A Survey of Japanese and foreign companies,* 1994.

Building on recent achievements

As noted, the progressive relaxation of the LSRS law in 1992 and 1994 eased entry barriers to retailing, thereby resulting in considerable structural change in this sector. While the revised LSRS law has reduced the power of small retailers, it still requires the LSRS Council to hold hearings with consumers, retailers and academic experts concerning the size of a new store before making recommendations to the Minister of International Trade and Industry. The Council and MITI have the authority to reduce the size of the planned store. Since 1992, however, the LSRS Council has imposed smaller reductions on the dimensions of new large stores (Table 34). As a result, the average size of new stores has increased. In certain cases, though, the LSRS Council has reduced the size of planned stores by over half. Moreover, the JFTC has reported that there are municipalities that have local regulations in addition to the national law. Some local authorities also appear to have tried to force supermarket chains to reduce the scale of development before lodging their application. There are, thus, still barriers to free competition in retail distribution.

The government has announced its intention to review the existing law. Liberalisation of the law has lowered prices by increasing competition among retailers and among manufacturers. The first effect was presumably predictable, but the growth of competition from private brands offered by supermarkets probably was not. The growth in inter-brand competition, based on imports and the production of smaller domestic manufacturers, suggests that the Japanese Fair Trade Commission should increase its surveillance of the various *keiretsu* relationships linking manufacturers, wholesalers and department stores. These relationships may, to a certain extent, amount to competition-restricting vertical restraints rather than merely being more efficient ways of doing business. Mean-

Table 34. **Average reduction in the size of development projects**

		1992[1]	1993	1994
Initial application	m^2	16 504	15 302	16 392
Permission granted	m^2	13 453	12 778	14 446
Reduction	per cent	18.5	16.5	11.9

1. The numbers for 1992 began on 31 January of that year when the new Large-Scale Retail Store law was implemented.
Source: Ministry of International Trade and Industry.

while, to maintain the momentum towards more competitive markets, the government should preferably aim to abolish restrictions on large stores by the end of the century, while preventing the introduction of new regulations at the local level. This could be accomplished by progressively increasing the lower limit at which the law is applied.

In addition to the constraints imposed by the LSRS law, liquor and tobacco distribution remains subject to some special regulations. In the March 1995 deregulation plan, a review of the requirements for obtaining a licence to sell liquor or tobacco was included in order to further lower entry barriers in distribution. For instance, for a store of less than 10 000 square metres to obtain a licence to sell liquor, it must be located at least 100 metres from other similar stores. In addition, the provision of new liquor licences is now based on population criteria. It is reported by the JFTC that only one-third of chain stores have been able to obtain a licence, suggesting that there is discrimination in favour of department stores. One objective of the regulation is to control the social costs resulting from the use of alcohol. A consequence of the regulation is that the balance between supply and demand remains in favour of retailers. Similar licensing arrangements apply to the sale of tobacco, which must be sold at a price approved by the government. Since 1985, though, approval of price changes, as well as the pricing of new products, has been automatic in principle.

While the reforms that have been enacted between 1990 and 1994 are beginning to lower prices in the retail sector, there are many other areas where there is scope to reduce prices closer to the levels found in other countries. A MITI survey of businessmen reported that entry and pricing regulations were a major cause of price differentials between Japan and the rest of the OECD, especially in energy and service industries (Figure 50). In the manufacturing and processing industries, on the other hand, regulations were seen as having little effect on prices, though standards and certification procedures were thought to have some impact.

Strong enforcement of anti-monopoly laws is required to ensure that deregulation increases competition and benefits consumers. Competition will be promoted by the JFTC's recommendations, such as in the case involving a cosmetics firm which had asked a major supermarket chain not to sell their products at a low price (the manufacturer having offered the supermarket samples of their products in exchange for leaving the prices unchanged). The JFTC decided that

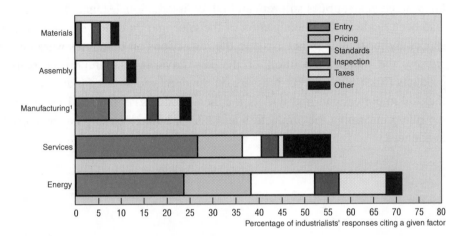

Figure 50. **GOVERNMENT REGULATIONS WHICH RAISE PRICES:**
THE PERCEPTIONS OF INDUSTRIALISTS

1. Manufacturing includes materials, assembly and energy.
Source: MITI, *A Survey of Japanese and foreign countries in terms of industrial intermediate goods and services.*

such behaviour constituted retail price maintenance, which is not allowed. The recent moves by the JFTC to examine the impact of government regulations on competition should also contribute to increasing competition.

Regulation appears to be at the origin of high prices in several service industries, including air transport, telecommunications, energy and postal services. There has been some progress in deregulating these areas. In *air transport*, a more transparent structure for setting international air fares was introduced in 1994. The regulations limiting discounts to certain categories of passengers were also liberalised. At the same time, a change in the regulations covering domestic airline prices to allow more competition and a generalisation of discount fares gave operators greater flexibility in determining their fare structures. However, there remains some partial entry barriers despite evidence that greater competition generates considerable increases in air traffic.[101]

As for *telecommunications*, the last major reform was introduced in 1985. It allowed more competition in various services, such as mobile telephone and international calls, but had little effect on core services such as local and inter-

117

urban calls. Although these reforms have allowed new entrants to gain a quarter of the international market, and resulted in a 50 per cent decline in prices during the past ten years, prices still remain high by international standards. Progress has also been made in the liberalisation of the telecommunication equipment market, especially for mobile phones, where the restrictions on purchases were ended. In *energy*, the planned abolition of the law covering the import of petroleum products in 1996 should put pressure on the domestic refining industry, provided that the importers can find outlets for their products. A modest liberalisation of the rules concerning the production and sale of bulk electricity has recently been announced.

V. Conclusions

After showing signs of recovery late in 1993, the Japanese economy slowed again at the end of 1994. Domestic demand benefited from rising public works expenditure and the income tax cuts which boosted consumption, while housing investment was stimulated by additional government loans and a further easing of monetary conditions. Moreover, after three consecutive years of decline, business investment stabilised in the middle of 1994, reflecting improved corporate profitability, especially in the manufacturing sector. During the initial upturn, exports increased as a result of the strength of the world economy. However, as most of the growth in demand was captured by imports, these also rose sharply in part because of expanding offshore production by Japanese companies in Asia – a trend that is likely to continue over the medium term. Overall, in 1994 as a whole, output grew by only $1/2$ per cent, and, by the second half of the year, unemployment rose to almost 3 per cent while inflation became negative.

In the first half of 1995, economic activity weakened further, with output falling somewhat. The renewed appreciation of the yen adversely affected business confidence. The household saving rate increased as unemployment rose and the deterioration in the real estate market persisted, while the demand for housing fell. Given the continued decline in output prices, there was growing concern about the health of the economy, which was accentuated by the failure of some financial institutions.

Macroeconomic policy has been geared towards preventing the continuation of such unfavourable developments. During the first half of 1994, money market conditions were substantially eased, but the stimulative effect of such a move was limited by banks' increased lending margins and the persistently faster-than-expected fall in inflation. After a short interruption in the second half of 1994, when the recovery seemed to be in motion, the monetary easing resumed at the beginning of 1995 as the appreciation of the yen lowered expectations of future growth. The Bank of Japan pushed down money market rates significantly, lowering its discount rate twice to 0.5 per cent by early September 1995. Later in the month, a new package was introduced by the government to stimulate the economy further. This package, amounting to Y 14 trillion (3 per cent of GDP), was aimed at ensuring a steady progression of public investment and providing increased availability of finance for housing and small businesses.

• These measures can be expected to revive the economy. The reduction in short-term interest rates should be reflected in increased domestic liquidity and lower financing costs for enterprises, which, together with a more competitive yen, might help restore business confidence. Consequently, private investment should increase significantly in 1996, accelerating later in the year as the impact of the lower value of the currency moderates the loss in export market shares. Timely implementation of the recent economic package should also add to the growth of domestic demand in 1996. Such developments may lead to an increase in household spending as consumers progressively regain the confidence which was lacking in 1995. As a result, while overall growth for 1995 may be barely positive, the economy should progressively strengthen during 1996, with growth perhaps averaging around 2 per cent.

• In the period immediately ahead, however, there remains some uncertainty about the strength of the recovery. One risk in this regard is that consumers might further increase their savings in response to bleak employment prospects. In addition, a persistent weakness of commercial land prices would risk exacerbating the balance-sheet problems of financial institutions, which, in turn, could adversely affect corporate confidence. Likewise, any renewed appreciation of the currency would inevitably worsen the business climate, possibly resulting in cuts in investment and an increased shift of production overseas, leading to additional falls in employment.

• Given these short-term risks, it is crucial that an easy monetary stance be maintained in order to support domestic demand and, hence, ensure a sustained recovery. Keeping monetary conditions easy would also have the advantage of improving asset market conditions and strengthening banks' balance sheets. However, such action alone would not be sufficient to restore stability in the financial system. Since the end of the 1980s, falling equity and real estate prices have undermined the capital base of deposit-taking institutions: according to most recent official estimates, these institutions held Y 40 trillion of non-performing loans (5.8 per cent of their total lending), some of which have already been provisioned or are backed by collateral which may be sold at reduced prices. While major banks are in the process of resolving their bad debt problem, it may take many years for a few of them to return to a healthy financial position. The problem appears to be even greater amongst second-tier regional banks as well as credit associations and agricultural co-operatives whose asset quality has deteriorated significantly. In addition, it appears that some mutually owned life insurance companies also have bad debts and may face difficulties in meeting the returns guaranteed to past savers.

To deal with such a situation specific actions are required. Three main options seem to be available to policy makers in this respect. One would be to continue the current policy of *forbearance*, in which supervisors tolerate accounting practices that allow time for banks to accumulate adequate reserves against bad loans. This policy has worked well for the major city banks, which are gradually completing their adjustment. It is not, however, well suited to smaller banks, including the second-tier regional banks, credit associations and agricultural co-operatives, some of which have proportionally larger bad debts and weak operating profits. These financial institutions would need a strong recovery in real estate prices, which seems highly uncertain. Another option, which was used by the authorities in the past, would consist of promoting *assisted mergers* between troubled financial institutions and other banks. In this regard, the Deposit Insurance Corporation has helped banks to take over the assets and liabilities of some ailing financial institutions. However, this approach is not always feasible since not all banks are in a position to participate in such operations. Hence, the need for a third option of using *public funds*.

Following the interim report of an advisory committee, the government is currently studying the modalities for coping with the difficulties of the financial sector. According to this report, the cost of liquidating a failed financial institution should first be met by using the deposit insurance system which would need to be strengthened. In addition, the report suggests that public money may have to be injected on a temporary basis. The Ministry of Finance has already set a number of conditions that must be fulfilled before deposit insurance can be used to guarantee the solvency of financial institutions. These are designed to ensure that the owners and management do not avoid losses as a result of bailouts while minimising problems of moral hazard in the future. With respect to the use of public money, the government intends to make some decisions on the basis of the final report of the advisory committee. It is also committed to introducing legislation designed to facilitate earlier action when financial institutions are in trouble and to set up a framework for raising funds from the private sector to participate in this action.

While any public involvement in the resolution of the difficulties facing troubled financial institutions would inevitably result in an increased debt-servicing burden for the public sector, the implications for the society at large would differ depending on the form it would take. Assistance provided by the Deposit Insurance Corporation might require a significant increase in the deposit insurance premium and borrowing for liquidity purposes by that institution, thus putting the burden on depositors and well-managed banks. On the other hand, financial support through the government budget would place the burden on taxpayers. Even capital injections from the Bank of Japan would have budgetary costs, as they would result in lower profits transferred by the Bank to the government. Consequently, the benefits of public intervention to restore a sound banking system would have to be set against the problems associated with moral hazard and the further widening of the budget deficit.

Between 1990 and 1995, there has been a substantial deterioration in public finances, with the combined central and local government balance swinging from approximate balance to a deficit of just under 8 per cent of GDP. The fiscal year 1994 budget reduced income taxes while cutting total expenditure by a small amount, although the delayed implementation of public works programmes kept actual spending on a rising track until the end of the calendar year. With a continued large social security surplus amounting to more than 3 per cent of GDP – part of which is used to finance the investment of local authorities and public corporations – the general government deficit is expected to be contained to 4 per cent of GDP in 1995. Since about half of this deficit is estimated to be structural in nature, the fiscal consolidation of the late 1980s appears to have been almost completely reversed.

The larger budget deficits have been reflected in a substantial increase in public debt with, as a result, interest payments now representing a significant portion of government expenditure. The ratio of gross general government debt to GDP rose from just under 70 per cent in 1991 to nearly 90 per cent in 1995, a level well above the OECD average. Though much lower, at 13 per cent of GDP, net debt is also rising significantly. A further deterioration of public finances is likely to result from the rapidly-ageing population, which should eventually turn the social security surplus into a deficit, and, as noted, from any possible bailout of depositors in ailing financial institutions. In view of these developments, it will be essential to implement a strong process of fiscal consolidation over the medium term. The legislated reform of the tax system should help in this respect through a rebalancing in the composition of revenues from direct to indirect taxation, as this will allow an increase in revenues from consumption taxes sufficient to compensate for the recently enacted income tax cuts. More generally, the presentation of overall public sector accounts to include government guarantees, loans and future contingent liabilities would also be useful, as this would increase the transparency of the current and prospective fiscal situation.

, If the economic situation remains weak, however, a degree of support would need to be maintained for a while. The preparedness of the authorities to prolong the temporary income tax cuts to 1996, if the recovery continues to be delayed, is welcome in this regard. The government will also need to reverse the current decline in public works expenditure. This should be achieved by the September 1995 package which will bring forward expenditure from the ten-year plan designed to improve public infrastructure and the quality of life. Careful attention, though, will have to be paid to the choice of projects in this area in order to obtain the maximum value for money, given that the allocation of funds for public works among different ministries has changed little over time. More generally, public expenditure will have to be carefully monitored in order to eliminate inefficient spending programmes.

, While macroeconomic policies, supplemented by public support to ailing financial institutions, would help initiate and consolidate the upturn, it will take time to complete the necessary adjustment of the economy. Ultimately, the key to sustaining growth in the medium term remains deregulation and, more broadly, structural reform. Progress in deregulation continued during 1994 with the implementation of several hundred measures included in government liberalisation packages, together with additional changes adopted as a result of the "framework talks" with the United States. The most important deregulation measures have taken place in financial markets. Following successive liberalisations of interest rates, restrictions on the introduction of new financial instruments will be eased while the management of pension funds and investment trusts will be partially opened to both domestic and foreign advisory companies. In the insurance market, regulations on products and rates will be gradually liberalised and a broker system will be introduced. Japan will also make changes in its public procurement procedures for telecommunications and medical technology in order to increase access for foreign firms. In autos and auto parts, the most contentious area of US-Japan consultations, the Japanese authorities decided to deregulate their auto inspection system while maintaining safety and environmental standards in this area. The two countries agreed not to establish official targets for purchases of foreign auto parts, though Japanese companies announced plans to continue expanding vehicle production abroad and increase imports.

Perhaps more important, though, than these incremental deregulation measures was the passage of the Administrative Procedures Law, which attempts to make the bureaucratic decision-making process more transparent and less arbitrary. Active enforcement of this law has the potential to alter substantially the relationship between the government and the private sector by reducing the scope for "administrative guidance". In addition, the Japan Fair Trade Commission has established guidelines to ensure that such guidance does not lead to practices conflicting with the Anti-Monopoly Act. Finally, the deregulation process itself has been made more transparent. The new five-year plan announced in March 1995, which was later shortened to three years, is based, in part, on the deregulation proposals submitted by domestic and foreign companies, as well as foreign governments. The plan will be reviewed each December on the basis of comments from interested parties and a revised version will be introduced the following March. In addition, a timetable has been attached to each proposal.

 Overall, however, the pace of deregulation continues to be slow and is unlikely to be significantly accelerated by the March 1995 programme. Some of the new measures commit the government only to review certain regulations, without indicating whether this will lead to their abolition or to more than minor changes. It would be important in this respect that the government follows the programme's guideline of "freedom in principle and regulation as the exception" in economic areas to eliminate, rather than merely relax, regulations on a large scale. As deregulation could reduce employment in certain areas, it would need to be accompanied by appropriate training schemes to allow the reinsertion of those losing jobs in the process. Moreover, as proposed in the 1993 "Hiraiwa Report", the implementation of the reform would be facilitated by the establishment of a powerful independent organisation to review the nearly 11 000 existing regulations and permits. The Administrative Reform Committee, which was created in December 1994, is supposed to operate as such an organisation. Finally, every new regulation should be subject to mandatory review after a limited period.

As discussed in the special chapter of the Survey, the retail distribution sector is one area where the relaxation of regulation in recent years has resulted in significant changes, both with respect to the provision of new services and price-setting behaviour. The distribution system in Japan consists of a large number of stores of relatively small size, with twice as many shops per person as in the United States or western Europe. The wholesale distribution framework is also considerably larger than elsewhere in the OECD area. Such a fragmented distribution sector has led to a level of productivity almost 30 per cent below the OECD average and, consequently, to final domestic prices for manufactured goods that are relatively high by international standards. To a certain extent, this appears to be the result of economic factors, such as high land prices which make storage expensive, thus favouring a dense network of shops. Nevertheless, regulations, including entry barriers for new stores that have tended to protect small traders and their employees, have lowered overall labour productivity.

The regulations governing the opening of new stores were liberalised with a new law introduced in 1992. The authorities are now only allowed one year to decide on an application for this purpose. In addition, the new law abolished the effective veto that existing retailers used to have over the opening of new stores. As a result, the rate at which new stores are created has markedly increased while the rate of closure of existing small stores more than doubled between 1991 and 1994. Other structural factors, such as more cost-conscious behaviour by consumers and the suburbanisation of the country, have also led to changes in the retail sector. Discount stores have taken advantage of these changes, as well as profiting from the expanded supply of low-cost imports from nearby Asian countries.

These developments have amplified the price declines generated by the weak macroeconomic environment and the yen appreciation. Preliminary empirical evidence suggests that costs in the distribution sector may be falling by 1 per cent per year faster than before the amendment of the law concerning large-scale retail stores. This would seem sufficient to raise consumers' income by approximately $50 billion ($\frac{3}{4}$ per cent of GDP) over a five-year period. Moreover, as the rate of new store openings is accelerating, the welfare gains are likely to increase in coming years.

Despite this progress, there is a need for further liberalisation, which would be beneficial for both consumers' real incomes and corporate sector costs. In the retail sector, the government should preferably aim to abolish restrictions on large stores by the end of the century, while preventing the introduction of new regulations at the local level. Anti-monopoly legislation would need to be tightly enforced to ensure that retailers enjoy full freedom in setting prices. The distribution of alcohol and tobacco should also be relaxed, while taking into account the social consequences of consumption of these products. Elsewhere in the service sector, price comparisons suggest that deregulation would be particularly helpful in reducing the cost of air travel, both domestic and international. Telecommunications is another area where competition could be increased for example, by lifting the NTT local network monopoly in order to reduce prices for inter-urban calls. Further action would be needed to lower the price of international communications. Finally, a major effort would be required to deregulate the distribution and production of energy in addition to the planned liberalisation of imports in this field.

In summary, the Japanese economy is experiencing an exceptionally long period of depressed activity, as hopes of a recovery, which were evident in early 1994, did not fully materialise. As a result, monetary policy has been further relaxed and a new economic package, including increased public works expenditure, was introduced in September 1995. While these measures, together with the recent depreciation of the yen, should help revive the economy, there are still uncertainties as to the strength of the upturn. This suggests the maintenance of an easy monetary stance, as well as the rapid implementation of a government programme, involving public money, to deal with the fragility of credit institutions. Although too rapid a reduction of the budget deficit would not be appropriate as long as the economy remains weak, there is a need for fiscal consolidation in the medium term given the already high government deficits and debt. The limited room for manoeuvre on the macropolicy side underlines the necessity for prompter action on deregulation, including a further liberalisation of the distribution system and a more vigorous enforcement of competition laws. This would contribute to making the Japanese market more open, accessible and efficient for domestic and foreign firms, while boosting the long-term productivity and growth prospects of the economy. It would also improve the welfare of the Japanese population and strengthen the international trading system.

Notes

1. Gross operating profits in the manufacturing sector were up 13 per cent (year-on-year) in the fourth quarter of 1994. During the past 25 years, profit margins have been closely correlated with capacity utilisation.

2. Despite a modest 2.5 per cent rise in depreciation, cash flow (operating profits plus depreciation and other non-operating income minus net interest costs) increased by 12 per cent between the fourth quarters of 1993 and 1994, as a result of higher operating profits and lower interest payments. Cash flow has been closely correlated with investment in the past.

3. The fall in business investment has allowed the ratio of the capital stock to potential output to return to its long-term trend level (Figure 5, Panel C). Business investment's share of GDP is low by historical standards. Growth at the potential rate of $2^1/_2$ per cent would imply an increase in the capital stock of about $3^1/_2$ per cent annually. As a result, the capital to output ratio would increase by only 1 per cent annually, considerably below its long-term trend of close to 2 per cent.

4. Foreign direct investment increased from 5.4 per cent of domestic business investment in FY 1993 to 6.2 per cent in FY 1994. This reflects a 14 per cent increase in the dollar value of overseas investment, which was concentrated in the manufacturing sector (see below).

5. In fact, the replacement cycle was expected to begin in 1993, but was delayed by poor economic conditions that year (EPA 1994).

6. According to a study by Moody's Investor Service, Japan's system of lifetime employment may impair the competitiveness and hence creditworthiness of some of its largest companies in such industries as banking, airlines, steel, chemicals, cement, paper and pulp. An Asahi Bank poll of 304 chief executive officers of Japanese companies found that 27 per cent believe that the lifetime employment practice is already collapsing and 64 per cent said the time to review the practice is approaching.

7. Conversely, the saving rate tends to rise with inflation, which erodes the purchasing power of funds already saved and increases the amount that households feel they need for retirement.

8. The maximum loan amount was reduced from 100 per cent of the cost of the house to 80 per cent and the waiting time for loans was increased.

9. The increased funding boosted the government's share of total housing loans to 40 per cent in 1994 compared with 34 per cent in 1990.

10. Temporary housing constructed by the government is included in housing starts but not in housing investment. It is included instead in public investment.

11. Scheduled labour hours declined from 1 859 in FY 1990 to 1 770 in FY 1994.

12. The indicator is defined as the difference between the percentage of firms replying that they have excess workers and those that face a shortage of workers.

13. The figure was substantially less for smaller manufacturing firms and non-manufacturing companies of all sizes. Only 13 per cent of small and medium-sized manufacturing enterprises and 7 per cent of non-manufacturing firms of all sizes reported having excess labour in May. All these figures, though, were higher than in the February Tankan survey.

14. The unemployment rate in Japan including discouraged and involuntary part-time workers was 5.7 per cent in 1993, about half of the OECD average of 10.8 per cent (OECD, *Employment Outlook*, July 1995).

15. The decline in agricultural employment had averaged 182 000 annually during the five years to 1993 before falling to 54 000 in 1994.

16. The fares on the underground and buses operated by the Tokyo city government were increased by 14 and 12 per cent, respectively, at the start of March, while a 9 per cent rise in taxi fares was authorised. In addition, fares in the privately-run Tokyo underground lines were increased by 16 per cent in May, while the fourteen major private railway companies have asked for permission to increase their fares by 20 per cent.

17. A similar gap between the rate of change in the prices of goods and services occurred at the wholesale level. The wholesale price index for services (known as the Corporate Services Index) has declined by less than that for goods. After increasing until 1993, it fell by just under 1 per cent in 1994 and at a slightly faster rate in the first half of 1995. In contrast, prices regulated by the government (financial services, passenger transport and communications), which account for almost one-fifth of the total index, increased 1.3 per cent in the year to March 1995. The current upward movement in administered service prices reflects the fact that they have been restrained during the past few years.

18. This measure uses relative consumer prices in a common currency.

19. Export prices have been measured using the relevant national accounts data which exclude the impact of quality improvement and the movement to higher value-added products. Consequently, they show a less rapid decline over time than do the customs-based data.

20. According to the EPA, the price elasticity of demand for Japanese exports fell from –1.1 in the period 1974 to 1985 to –0.3 in the period 1985 to 1992 (EPA, 1993).

21. According to one estimate, the price elasticity of import demand increased from –0.3 in 1992 to –0.4 at the end of 1994, while income elasticity rose from 1.4 to 1.7 over the same period (Salomon Brothers, 1995).

22. According to estimates by the EPA, the price and income elasticities for imports of consumer goods are –0.9 and 1.9, respectively, compared to only –0.6 and 1.2 for capital goods and –0.1 and 0.9 for industrial supplies (EPA, 1992).

23. EPA, *Survey of Japan*, p. 269.

24. This motivation was cited by only 2 per cent of the firms investing in the United States and the European Union. This survey by the Export-Import Bank of Japan was cited in *Foreign Direct Investment in East Asia*, (Japan Institute for Overseas Investment), May 1993.

25. ''Overseas Investment Statistics Compilation'', MITI.

26. The same survey reported that about 15 per cent of Japanese firms cited trade barriers as the main reason for investing in the United States and Europe. In the case of ASEAN, this motivation was cited only by 3 per cent of the firms.

27. If the petroleum and coal product industries are excluded, the share of overseas production by US firms was 18 per cent. The share of manufacturing output in the United States by foreign-owned entities rose from 10 per cent in 1987 to 14 per cent in 1992. Japanese firms accounted for about 13 per cent of this output.

28. The size and even sign of the real interest rate differentials depends on which price index is used. The above calculations use the least volatile components of the CPI and so exclude food and energy prices. If the domestic wholesale price had been used, the real long-term differential would have remained positive during 1994 and widened in 1995, so supporting the yen.

29. The regulations covering foreign currency lending by insurance companies were liberalised; the limit on the share of yen-denominated loans in total external lending was abolished; the regulation governing the period during which offshore yen bonds could not be sold in Japan was also removed, while the foreign exchange limits on banks were separated between currency and bond positions. In addition, institutional investors were given more scope to decide on the appropriate valuation method for foreign bonds.

30. This resulted in a deceleration in the growth of M3+CD despite the increase in postal deposits and money trusts, which are included in that aggregate.

31. City banks, long-term credit banks and trust banks.

32. Credit institutions are defined as all private deposit-taking institutions plus private non-bank credit institutions.

33. Loans that are at least six months overdue or loans to legally bankrupt companies. The rules governing the classification of loans as non-performing vary across countries. The principal difference between current Japanese rules and those in the United States is that restructured loans – where the initial terms have been changed to reduce or exempt the interest payment obligations or where the interest payments have been suspended – are not disclosed in Japan while they are in the United States. As from March 1996, the 21 major banks will start disclosing the amount of their restructured loans.

34. For the major banks, 45 per cent of unrealised securities gains, which are included in Tier 2 of net worth, decreased Y 5.1 trillion, more than the decrease in total net worth, Y 3.9 trillion.

35. The core capital excludes equity shareholdings and subordinated debt.

36. In February, banks sold loans to the CCPC at 34 per cent of their face value. In July 1995, the Ministry of Finance suggested that the residual value of problem loans was 40 per cent of their face value.

37. In many cases the revaluation does not require that banks permanently sell their shares. Rather they are sold and repurchased. This has the effect of revaluing the holding and passing a realised gain through the profit and loss account without changing the underlying worth of the bank at all.

38. The agricultural co-operative banking system has three levels: a national bank, federations of co-operatives covering one prefecture and local co-operatives.

39. The only information available on the extent of the non-performing loans of regional banks is the amount of their credits to bankrupt companies. In the case of major banks, such lending represents 0.6 per cent of loans, while it was only 0.5 per cent for first-tier regional banks in September 1994. For second-tier banks, though, the ratio was 1.0 per cent.

40. If a credit co-operative operates in two, or more, prefectures, it is supervised by the Ministry of Finance. Few associations, however, fall into this category.

41. One early warning sign of the crisis was that the two credit unions, "Tokyo Kyowa Credit Co-operative" and "Anzen Credit Co-operative", were offering deposit rates considerably higher than the market average. A new bank, "Tokyo Kyodo Bank", was created to which all assets and liabilities were transferred. It started operation at the end of March 1995 with financial contributions from the Bank of Japan (Y 20 billion in capital), private banks (Y 20 billion in capital and Y 30 billion in income support), Deposit Insurance Corporation (Y 40 billion in income support), Association of Credit Co-operatives (Y 15 billion in income support) and the Long-Term Credit Bank of Japan (Y 20 billion in income support). The Tokyo Metropolitan Government has not yet approved its planned contribution (Y 30 billion in income support).

42. Under restructuring plans implemented since March 1993, agricultural co-operatives have earned interest payments of 4.5 per cent, other financial institutions 2.5 per cent while parent institutions have received zero interest.

43. Moreover, the discount to face value offered to the CCPC by vendors has grown from 34 per cent in March 1993 to 63 per cent in March 1995.

44. This includes only realised gains and losses. In particular, insurance companies have experienced exchange-rate losses on their uncovered foreign-currency bonds.

45. The duration of the average policy is seven years.

46. The DIC was established in 1971 with a capital of Y 455 million (Y 155 million from private financial institutions, Y 150 million from the government and Y 150 million from the Bank of Japan). It covers all banks, shinkin banks, credit and labour co-operatives. The corporation had resources of Y 896 billion at the end of March 1995 and in addition, had a credit line of Y 500 billion at the Bank of Japan. It charges a premium of 0.012 per cent of deposits which are insured to a limit of Y 10 million.

47. The SDIC was established in 1973 with a capital of Y 300 million. It covers agricultural and fishery co-operatives. The corporation had resources of Y 106 billion at the end of March 1995 with a combined credit line of Y 100 billion at the Norinchukin Bank and the Bank of Japan. Its charges and insurance of deposits are the same as those of the DIC.

48. The surplus represents an accumulation of funds designed to smooth the future path of contributions.

49. It is not possible to give the increases for the net credit extended to these sectors. The figures are gross of loan repayments.

50. At the time when the plan was announced the last official estimates for public investment expenditure were for FY 1992.

51. The most important change was the end of the ban on Japanese and foreign lawyers sharing offices. The legislation also gave the Ministry of Justice more leeway in setting experience requirements. These changes went into effect in June 1995.

52. Under the old legislation, consumers had to prove negligence on the part of manufacturers in order to claim compensation. Under the new law consumers must prove only that a product is defective and that they thereby have suffered injury.

53. Japanese laws are usually vague and leave much room for manoeuvre by the ministries or agencies charged with drafting implementing regulations and overseeing their application.

54. In total, 3 400 comments were received of which about 1 750 were relevant to deregulation. About 200 of these proposals were based on incorrect information. The six governments submitting comments were Australia, Canada, Germany, Korea, the United Kingdom and the United States.

55. *The Japan Times*, 1 April 1995, p. 12. For example, Keidenren, the leading Japanese business group, submitted 456 deregulation requests of which 131 were included in the package.

56. These comments will be channelled through a non-government Administrative Reform Promotion Headquarters. In addition, each ministry will establish an office to receive opinions and requests from interested parties, both domestic and foreign.

57. This may reflect consumer preference for American grain-fed beef rather than the less expensive grass-fed beef from Australia.

58. The Pension Welfare Service Public Corporation, which manages part of the Employees' Pension Insurance Pension Fund and the National Pension Fund, was permitted to use investment advisory companies beginning in FY 1995, as was the portion of the National Public Service Mutual Aid Associations which is managed on a discretionary basis.

59. Foreign fund managers have complained that accounting and reporting rules on a historical cost and accrual basis obscured their superior performance.

60. The United States provides national treatment on a MFN basis. However, Japanese firms operating in the United States have been concerned that the "Fair Trade in Financial Services" Act, which mandates reciprocal, rather than national, treatment might be enacted by the US Congress.

61. These measures, perhaps the most important in this sector since the 1984 Yen-Dollar agreement, had created hopes of advancing the multilateral financial services talks held under the Uruguay Round. These expectations were disappointed, though, when the United States rejected the offers of developing countries as insufficient in June 1995.

62. The proposals to liberalise insurance products and rates and to introduce a broker system were included in the July 1994 deregulation plan.

63. According to a study by *Yomiuri Shimbun*, which was cited in *Nihon Keizai Shimbun*, 1 June 1995, six of the ten non-life insurance companies surveyed have decided to start life

insurance companies. However, only two life insurance companies plan to enter the non-life insurance business.

64. This includes only purchases above 100 000 SDRs, a threshold which also applies to the figure of medical technology purchases cited below.

65. An existing procurement pact with NTT was also modified and extended. Although NTT was officially privatised in 1985, the government still owns 65 per cent of it.

66. Moreover, patent applications are open for public inspection eighteen months after submission.

67. Some foreign firms have complained that their patent applications have been held up by the burden of countering a barrage of opposition filings from Japanese firms.

68. First, all patent applications will be opened for public inspection eighteen months after submission. Second, a patent's duration will be limited to twenty years from the date of application instead of seventeen years from the date that it is granted. Third, the process of protesting patents, which some foreign firms had complained was too difficult, will be eased. Fourth, dependent patent compulsory licences will only be granted when necessary to remedy a practice determined to be anti-competitive or to permit public non-commercial use. Despite these measures to harmonise the two countries patent systems, significant differences remain. Most importantly, the United States continues to use the first-to-invent system, which gives the right to file a patent to the person who first publicly announces an invention. Japan, as well as most other countries, gives priority on a first-to-file basis.

69. Asahi Glass Co., Ltd., Nippon Sheet Glass Co., Ltd. and the Central Glass Co., Ltd.

70. These include encouraging US manufacturers to respond to Japanese user and distributor requirements, to understand the Japanese business environment and to hold annual trade shows in Japan.

71. In May 1995, the United States made a positive finding against Japan's market for replacement auto parts under Section 301 of its Trade Act and announced its intention to impose 100 per cent duties on $5.9 billion of Japanese luxury car exports. In response, Japan requested consultations at the World Trade Organisation.

72. In January 1992, the Japanese Government noted that Japanese car producers had a goal of purchasing $19 billion of American-made parts in FY 1994. This figure, which was based on the plans of individual car producers, included $15 billion for their North American operations and $4 billion of imports for production in Japan. In fact, Japanese car producers purchased $19.9 billion of American-made parts in FY 1994. Imports to Japan though, accounted for only $3 billion of this total, reflecting declining auto production in Japan.

73. The US government believes that the system of multi-brand dealerships in the United States was instrumental in allowing the Japanese car producers to capture a large market share and that the same system should exist in Japan. It should be noted, though, that some European car manufacturers have built their own dealership networks at a high cost. Exclusive dealership networks are still allowed in the European Union under an exemption from competition laws.

74. The US Government had initially requested that Japan separate the repair shops from the inspection facilities in order to loosen the grip of Japanese manufacturers on the supply of replacement parts to garages.

75. The period allowed for review, though, may reflect the time needed to build a consensus for change.

76. In contrast, the deregulation process in the United States, for example, has focused on the liberalisation of sectors thought to have been natural monopolies, such as airlines and telecommunications. This may explain the difference with Japan, where deregulation has been primarily a gradual scaling back of the government's pervasive role in the economy.

77. Measured at factor cost.

78. The employment measure, though, makes no distinction between full and part-time employment, which may differ across countries.

79. The purchasing power parity has been calculated by separating retail service items from retail sales of goods. This parity uses prices for final goods sales, which may not be appropriate for value-added comparisons.

80. The German data refers to enterprises and so some small shops may be hidden in the figures for large enterprises.

81. According to Tsurata and Yatagi (1991, p. 305), one supermarket firm estimated that 35 per cent of the cost of a 10 000 square metre supermarket ($685 000) consisted of these ''negotiation'' payments.

82. Flath, *Japan and the World Economy* (1990); Nishimura and Tachibana, *Essays in Japanese Economy* (1995).

83. Flath showed that the cross-prefectoral differences in the number of shops is negatively affected by car ownership and population density and positively influenced by living space.

84. Nishimura, *op. cit.*, p. 3. There appeared to be no impact on smaller stores (500 to 1 500 square metres) perhaps due to the fact that the research was based on 1985 data and this type of store had only been regulated since 1979.

85. Most small stores are part of the owner's house. The inheritance tax treats land (up to lots of 200 square metres) more favourably than other assets.

86. OECD (mimeo), ''Structure and change in distribution systems'', forthcoming.

87. The economic factors were car density, urban concentration, population density, land price, female labour force participation and consumption.

88. The cutoff point for local decision making is 6 000 square metres in the major metropolitan areas.

89. This data refers to applications by the store developer under Article III of the LSRS law, which corresponds to the first line of Figure 39.

90. The ''shop within a shop'' selling format is also used in department stores in other countries.

91. This unit value index is calculated by the Seibu supermarket chain. The value of sales in a large number of different product categories is divided by the number of items sold.

92. For domestically-produced goods sold on the domestic market.

93. There is strong econometric evidence from the two recessions during the 1980s indicating that expectations play a key role in determining prices. The relationship between consumer price inflation and unemployment has been closer than that between the GDP deflator and unemployment because consumer prices depend on external factors, such as the exchange rate. The recessions in the 1980s were associated with appreciations of the exchange rate, which added to the slowdown in domestic prices through falls in import prices.

94. For the methodology used by the Secretariat in estimating potential growth and spare capacity, see OECD Economics Department *Working Paper No. 152.*

95. This is consistent with the pioneering study by Kravis, Heston and Summers in 1978 (*International comparisons of real product and purchasing power*) which found a clear and positive relationship between the prices of goods and services and the level of income across a wide range of countries. The dispersion of prices across countries was the least for manufactured goods and greatest in education, transport and government services.

96. The relative price levels are taken from the 1993 OECD Purchasing Power Parity study and are based on a special aggregation of data compiled by the EKS method. Health services have been excluded from both private and public services due to the markedly different pricing and subsidy arrangements for these services in different OECD countries. Food has been excluded from the goods component because of the wide variation in protection and subsidy policies in the OECD area.

97. This relationship has been quite stable over time, fluctuating between 70 and 80 per cent between 1975 and 1993.

98. Price differentials also reflect differences in indirect tax rates. These are relatively low in Japan and the United States compared with other OECD countries. Prices of petroleum products also differ for tax reasons and thus may also bias the comparison.

99. Such calculations require international price data for intermediate inputs, which are not readily available. Moreover, the higher the share of intermediate output in gross output the more errors are likely when calculating relative price levels based on value-added factors for different industries.

100. Pilat, 1993.

101. Between 1986 and 1989, the addition of a second company on eight domestic routes generated a more than 30 per cent increase in traffic in the following year.

The March 1995 deregulation plan

As indicated in Chapter III of the main text, a deregulation plan for the five-year period FY 1995 to FY 1999 was announced on 31 March 1995. The plan was later compressed to three years in response to the sharp appreciation of the yen in April. It contains 1 091 measures in eleven areas. The major changes planned and the objectives in each area are briefly summarised below.

1. Housing and land (86 measures)

Regulations on land use and land/building ratios will be relaxed in order to encourage the effective use of land. The objectives are to facilitate the supply of land for building, increase the availability of high-quality housing and reduce housing construction costs.

2. Information and telecommunications (53 measures)

There will be a comprehensive review of the existing legal system governing telecommunications, broadcasting and cable television to take account of the growing degree of overlap between these three industries. Regulations on entry to Type I telecommunications business (firms that own their own networks), as well as on prices and services offered, will be examined with the goal of making them more transparent. The easing of regulations is intended to make the benefits of advances in information technology more widely available and promote the creation of new businesses.

3. The distribution system (120 measures)

The Large-Scale Retail Store Law and the requirements for obtaining a liquor sales license will be reviewed. These additional reforms in the retail system are intended to reduce distribution costs and narrow the price differentials between Japan and other countries.

4. Transportation (168 measures)

Regulations related to the truck and warehousing industries will be eased. The auto inspection system will be relaxed to reduce the cost and burden on owners. For example, the six-month inspection will be abolished as will the requirement to have repairs done prior to inspection.

5. Standards, certification and import processing (240 measures)

The system of standards and certifications will be revised in line with international norms for many products, including construction materials, electrical appliances, food pharmaceuticals and motor vehicles. Customs clearance procedures will be further simplified and speeded-up. The measures in this area are intended to improve market access for imports.

6. Financial services and insurance (83 measures)

Many measures stemming from the negotiations with the United States under the *Japan-United States Framework for a New Economic Partnership*, such as liberalisation of the management of the National Employee's Pension Fund, the abolition of the waiting period on the sale of Euroyen bonds in Japan and the introduction of an insurance broker system, are included in this category.

7. Energy (26 measures)

The most important change in this area is the expiration in March 1996 of the law restricting imports of refined petroleum products. This will help make the energy supply system more flexible and efficient while reducing prices.

8. Employment and labour (30 measures)

Some of the regulations concerning the recruitment of labour will be abolished while rules related to working time, such as overtime and night-time work by women, will be reviewed. These measures are intended to ensure the welfare of workers.

9. Environmental protection (15 measures)

The administration of some laws aimed at preventing air pollution will be shifted from the central government to the prefectoral level, while environmental inspections by

MITI and local governments will be co-ordinated. The regulations limiting which companies are allowed to dispose of industrial waste will be eased.

10. Public safety and disaster prevention (131 measures)

The rules prohibiting self-service petrol stations will be discussed. Other measures concern such areas as high-pressure gases, explosives and fire prevention.

11. Other (139 measures)

Measures included in this category cover a wide range of topics, including health and medicine, education and scientific research. The rules covering the establishment of medical corporations will be simplified and policies to expand the medical treatment of patients in their own homes will be studied. There will also be changes in rules covering the use of DNA technology.

Annex II

Chronology of main economic events

1994

October

The cabinet decides on a tax reform package, consisting of a temporary reduction of income and residential taxes for two consecutive years from 1995 and a permanent taxation reform followed by an increase in consumption tax rates in 1997.

The government decides on the "Public Investment Basic Plan", which sets a target of about Y 630 trillion of public investment during fiscal years 1995 to 2004, with 60 to 64 per cent of funds to be allocated to raising living standards and improving welfare and cultural facilities.

November

The Economic Planning Agency formally announces that the latest economic recession, starting in April 1991, bottomed out in October 1993.

The Diet approves the tax reforms.

December

An agreement by the Bank of Japan, private financial institutions, and the Tokyo local government to establish a new bank to take over the assets and liabilities of Tokyo Kyowa Credit Association and Anzen Credit Association is announced.

The cabinet decides on an official economic projection of 2.8 per cent for FY 1995.

The Diet adopts the first supplementary budget for FY 1994.

The Cabinet approves the initial FY 1995 draft budget, featuring total expenditure of Y 71 trillion, a 2.9 per cent decrease over the initial budget for FY 1994.

1995

January

Japan and the US reach a conclusion on the liberalisation of financial services, which had been under discussion since September 1993.

A large-scale earthquake heavily damages the Hanshin-Awaji area, resulting in more than five thousand deaths and damage of about Y 10 trillion.

February

The Diet adopts the second supplementary budget for FY 1994, which amounts to Y 1 trillion, dealing especially with the damage caused by the Hanshin-Awaji Earthquake.

March

The Diet adopts the FY 1995 initial budget.

The government announces an interim report on economic deregulation measures for the coming five fiscal years.

The Bank of Japan announces its decision to ensure a decline in money market rates through open-market operations.

April

The government announces a package of emergency measures to deal with the consequences of the yen's appreciation.

The Bank of Japan cuts the official discount rate by 75 basis points to 1 per cent.

The yen passes above the 80 yen/dollar level for the first time.

May

The Diet passes the Law on the Decentralisation of Power.

The Diet adopts the first supplementary budget for FY 1995, amounting to Y 2.7 trillion.

June

The Ministry of Finance announces its guiding principles for reorganising the financial system.

The US and Japan bilateral talks on autos and auto parts reach a conclusion with the announcement of global business plans by Japanese auto companies, which aim at increasing overseas auto production and the purchase of competitive foreign auto parts.

July

The Product Liability Law takes effect.

The Bank of Japan announces its decision to encourage a decline in money market rates somewhat below the official discount rate.

The Tokyo Metropolitan Government orders Cosmo Credit Cooperative to suspend operations involving new loans and deposits.

August

The Ministry of Finance, aiming at curbing the yen's appreciation, announces a package of measures which ease restrictions on overseas investment and loans by institutional investors.

The Osaka Prefectural Government orders Kizu Credit Cooperative to suspend operations.

The Bank of Japan announces a plan for the liquidation of Hyogo Bank and the establishment of a new bank.

September

The Bank of Japan cuts the official discount rate by 50 basis points to 0.5 per cent.

The government announces a package of economic measures worth a total of Y 14.22 trillion.

The Financial System Stabilization Committee of the Financial System Research Council, an advisory committee of the Ministry of Finance, releases an interim report on measures facilitating the early settlement of non-performing loans of financial institutions.

October

The Diet adopts the second supplementary budget for FY 1995, amounting to Y 5.3 trillion.

STATISTICAL ANNEX AND STRUCTURAL INDICATORS

Table A. **Selected background statistics**

	Average 1985-94	1985	1986	1987	1988	1989	1990	1991	1992	1993	1994
A. Percentage change in constant 1985 prices											
Private consumption	3.2	3.4	3.4	4.2	5.2	4.3	3.9	2.2	1.7	1.0	2.2
Gross fixed capital formation	4.8	5.3	4.8	9.6	11.9	9.3	8.8	3.7	-1.1	-1.8	-2.4
Public investment	5.3	-6.6	3.6	7.3	5.2	-2.2	4.5	4.7	15.3	16.5	5.0
Residential construction	4.7	2.6	7.8	22.6	11.9	0.5	4.7	-8.2	-6.7	2.5	9.7
Private non-residential	5.0	12.1	4.4	6.7	14.8	16.6	11.4	6.6	-4.7	-9.3	-8.9
GDP at market prices	3.3	5.0	2.6	4.1	6.2	4.7	4.8	4.3	1.1	-0.2	0.5
GDP price deflator	1.2	1.6	1.8	0	0.4	1.9	2.2	2.0	1.5	0.8	0.2
Industrial production	1.9	3.8	-0.3	3.4	10.5	5.9	4.1	1.8	-6.1	-4.5	0.8
Employment	1.1	0.7	0.8	1.0	1.7	2.0	2.0	1.9	1.1	0.2	0.1
Compensation of employees (current prices)	5.1	4.7	4.7	3.9	5.9	7.4	8.6	7.8	3.7	2.3	2.3
Productivity (GDP/employment)	2.1	4.2	1.8	3.1	4.5	2.7	2.8	2.3	0	-0.4	0.5
Unit labour costs (compensation/GDP)	1.8	-0.3	2.0	-0.2	-0.3	2.5	3.6	3.4	2.5	2.5	1.8
B. Percentage ratios											
Gross fixed capital formation as per cent of GDP at constant prices	31.2	27.5	28.1	29.5	31.1	32.5	33.7	33.5	32.8	32.3	31.3
Stockbuilding as per cent of GDP at constant prices	0.6	0.7	0.5	0.3	0.8	1.0	0.7	0.9	0.4	0.2	0.4
Foreign balance as per cent of GDP at current prices	2.4	3.4	4.0	3.2	2.3	1.4	0.7	1.8	2.4	2.3	2.1
Compensation of employees as per cent of GDP at current prices	55.4	54.2	54.4	54.3	53.9	54.3	55.0	55.8	56.4	57.3	58.3
Direct taxes as per cent of household income	8.2	7.4	7.6	8.0	8.0	8.0	8.9	9.4	8.9	8.3	7.7
Household saving as per cent of disposable income	14.9	15.6	16.1	14.7	14.3	14.6	14.1	15.1	15.0	14.7	15.2
Unemployment rate	2.5	2.6	2.8	2.9	2.5	2.3	2.1	2.1	2.2	2.5	2.9
C. Other indicator											
Current balance (billion US dollars)	84.6	49.2	85.8	87.0	79.6	57.2	35.8	72.9	117.6	131.4	129.1

Source: OECD.

144

Table D. **Net domestic product by industry of origin**

Billion yen, current prices

	1985	1986	1987	1988	1989	1990	1991	1992	1993
Agriculture, forestry and fishing	8 348	8 072	7 968	7 918	8 265	8 770	8 661	8 381	8 340
Mining and quarring	758	794	781	852	828	1 039	1 024	1 057	986
Manufacturing	82 671	83 426	85 889	92 554	98 978	106 447	113 480	110 683	105 437
Construction	23 327	24 669	27 738	31 254	34 864	38 746	41 323	42 305	43 176
Electricity, gas and water	6 907	7 725	7 455	7 288	6 900	6 617	7 363	7 915	8 386
Wholesale and retail trade	39 869	40 419	42 295	44 565	46 400	50 217	52 614	53 803	53 144
Bank, insurance and real estate	39 819	42 467	46 121	49 997	54 207	55 529	56 894	57 949	58 251
Government services	24 207	25 391	26 098	26 989	28 389	30 180	31 697	33 037	34 033
Other services	64 155	68 212	70 821	74 763	81 129	88 009	92 542	96 095	98 105
Total	290 061	301 175	315 166	336 180	359 960	385 554	405 598	411 225	409 858
Import tax	1 353	1 046	1 166	1 217	2 252	2 713	2 872	2 887	2 549
Imputed rent	-14 774	-13 938	-15 677	-16 568	-20 450	-22 322	-22 670	-23 061	-20 720
Other[1]	..	..	..	..	-1 467	-2 209	-2 312	-2 021	-1 825
Net domestic product at factor cost	276 640	288 283	300 655	320 829	340 295	363 736	383 488	389 030	389 862

1. General consumption tax adjustment for investment expenditure.
Source: EPA, Annual Report on National Accounts; OECD, National Accounts.

147

Table E. **The distribution of national income**

Billion yen

	1985	1986	1987	1988	1989	1990	1991	1992	1993
GNP	321 556	335 838	350 479	373 731	399 046	427 469	454 487	467 413	470 353
(Taxes – Subsidies)[1]	21 411	21 694	23 869	25 761	27 017	28 546	30 540	35 492	36 486
GNP at factor cost	300 145	314 144	326 610	347 970	372 029	398 923	423 947	431 921	433 867
Depreciation	43 615	46 170	48 861	52 306	57 941	62 820	68 387	72 622	73 348
NNP at factor cost[2] (A)	256 530	267 974	277 749	295 664	314 088	336 103	355 560	359 299	360 519
Compensation of employees (B)	173 815	182 005	189 125	200 193	214 955	233 507	251 781	261 046	267 152
Operating surplus [= (A) – (B)]	82 715	85 969	88 624	95 471	99 133	102 596	103 779	98 253	93 367
Dividends, interest, rent, etc.[3]	24 483	26 258	25 586	26 249	30 332	37 525	43 207	39 136	37 059
Income of enterprises[3]	58 232	59 711	63 038	69 222	68 801	65 071	60 572	59 117	56 308
Private corporations[4]	28 273	29 178	31 018	36 051	32 623	30 242	29 302	24 772	26 264
Public enterprises	–166	–420	–256	–135	3 101	4 282	1 377	1 144	–1 308
Self employment[5]	30 124	30 953	32 276	33 306	33 077	30 548	29 894	33 201	31 352
Memorandum items:									
Total property income	40 921	43 455	43 284	44 471	49 220	57 997	65 162	61 139	58 699
of which:									
Paid by government and households	15 537	16 272	16 767	17 300	17 924	19 272	20 545	20 637	20 284

1. Includes the statistical discrepancy.
2. National income.
3. Operating surplus = Dividends, etc. + Income of enterprises.
4. After dividends payments.
5. Personal companies.
Source: EPA, *Annual Report on National Accounts;* OECD, *National Accounts.*

Table F. **Income and expenditure of households**

Billion yen

	1983	1984	1985	1986	1987	1988	1989	1990	1991	1992	1993
Compensation of employees	157 299	166 026	173 815	182 006	189 125	200 192	214 957	233 508	251 781	261 046	267 152
Wages and salaries	137 697	145 380	151 291	157 803	162 580	172 235	184 623	200 094	215 836	225 420	229 879
Employers' contribution to Social Security	11 615	12 360	13 437	14 610	15 376	16 258	17 759	20 067	21 421	22 556	23 521
Others	7 987	8 286	9 087	9 593	11 169	11 699	12 575	13 347	14 524	13 070	13 752
Income from property and entrepreneurship	53 814	55 894	60 222	62 430	62 997	63 994	67 736	71 512	75 146	75 455	71 634
Income from independent traders	35 712	37 352	40 890	42 092	43 901	45 290	45 687	46 626	47 559	49 845	46 543
Property income received, net	18 102	18 542	19 332	20 338	19 096	18 704	22 049	24 886	27 587	25 610	25 091
Current transfers from Government	33 234	34 524	36 709	39 471	42 533	44 548	46 153	51 308	52 203	55 767	58 862
Other transfers	15 718	16 127	16 655	17 288	17 705	18 995	18 920	20 192	22 412	23 544	23 541
Household income	260 065	272 571	287 401	301 195	312 360	327 729	347 766	376 520	401 542	415 812	421 189
less: Direct taxes on households and private non-profit institutions	19 470	20 323	21 248	22 995	25 098	26 268	27 925	33 355	37 650	37 039	34 865
less: Current transfers to Government	23 156	24 524	26 437	28 037	30 015	31 684	33 706	39 316	41 665	43 866	45 789
less: Other transfers	17 852	18 272	19 061	19 832	20 519	22 064	22 254	23 883	26 065	27 437	27 330
Disposable income	199 587	209 452	220 655	230 331	236 728	247 713	263 881	279 966	296 162	307 470	313 205
less: Consumption expenditure	167 509	176 267	186 235	193 308	201 973	212 237	225 427	240 493	251 540	261 201	267 125
Food	39 137	40 193	41 537	42 043	42 825	43 888	46 091	48 877	51 213	52 327	52 636
Clothing	11 458	11 925	12 491	12 873	13 374	13 549	14 289	15 287	16 123	15 703	15 272
Rent	30 949	32 994	35 082	36 113	37 919	40 036	42 751	45 953	49 080	52 095	54 976
Other	85 965	91 155	97 125	102 279	107 855	114 764	122 296	130 376	135 124	141 076	144 241
Household saving	32 079	33 185	34 421	37 022	34 755	35 475	38 454	39 473	44 621	46 269	46 080
(Per cent of disposable income)	16.1	15.8	15.6	16.1	14.7	14.3	14.6	14.1	15.1	15.0	14.7

Source: EPA, *Annual Report on National Accounts*; OECD, *National Accounts.*

149

Table G. **Appropriation account for general government**

Billion yen

	1985	1986	1987	1988	1989	1990	1991	1992	1993
Receipts:									
1. Direct tax	38 485	40 639	44 614	48 329	53 901	58 367	62 253	59 519	54 757
2. Social security contributions	26 185	27 761	29 694	31 363	33 387	38 957	41 264	43 436	45 331
3. Other current transfers received	826	901	1 027	1 091	1 173	1 298	1 419	1 533	1 593
4. Indirect taxes	24 900	25 213	28 379	30 878	32 162	35 212	34 968	37 301	37 199
5. Property income	8 369	9 346	10 009	11 112	11 617	13 188	15 119	14 582	14 640
6. Current receipts, total	98 765	103 860	113 723	122 773	132 240	147 022	155 023	156 371	153 520
Disbursements:									
7. Expenditure on goods and services	30 685	32 388	32 975	34 184	36 275	38 807	41 232	43 258	44 666
8. Property income payable	14 318	14 912	15 346	15 671	16 023	16 820	17 377	17 733	17 724
(Interest on public debt)	3 650	3 678	3 419	3 409	3 104	4 644	3 852	3 304	3 475
9. Subsidies	34 917	37 549	40 420	42 235	43 766	48 823	49 587	53 142	56 537
10. Social security outlays	1 539	1 615	1 716	1 854	2 047	2 239	2 527	2 794	3 037
11. Other current transfers paid	85 109	90 142	93 876	97 353	101 215	111 334	114 576	120 232	125 439
12. Current disbursements, total	13 655	13 718	19 848	25 420	31 025	35 688	40 447	36 138	28 081
13. Saving (6 – 12)	15 168	16 048	17 536	18 860	19 808	21 549	23 125	26 449	30 803
14. Gross investment	-465	-165	271	530	216	224	-1 357	404	-228
15. Net capital transfers received	2 078	2 144	2 245	2 325	2 458	2 508	2 525	2 624	2 779
16. Consumption of fixed capital	2 703	2 781	3 220	3 829	3 928	4 530	5 164	5 883	6 272
17. Other capital account items	-2 604	-3 131	1 607	5 586	9 964	12 342	13 326	6 834	-6 443
18. Net lending (13 – 14 + 15 + 16 – 17)									

Source: EPA, *Annual Report on National Accounts.*

Table H. **Appropriation account for public enterprises**

Billion yen

	1985	1986	1987	1988	1989	1990	1991	1992	1993
Receipts:									
Operating surplus	2 972	3 187	3 447	3 566	5 224	5 946	4 224	3 859	3 286
Property income	26 249	27 546	28 514	29 494	31 071	33 357	36 645	39 104	40 715
Current receipts, total	29 221	30 733	31 961	33 060	36 295	39 303	40 869	42 963	44 000
Disbursements:									
Direct taxes	1 658	1 437	745	328	335	247	1 094	2 492	1 856
Property income payable	29 386	31 153	32 217	33 195	33 194	35 022	39 492	41 819	45 308
Other current transfers, net	200	304	413	321	285	319	296	323	357
Current disbursements, total	31 244	32 894	33 375	33 843	33 814	35 587	40 883	44 634	47 521
Saving	-2 023	-2 161	-1 414	-784	2 481	3 716	-14	-1 671	-3 521
Memorandum items:									
Non-residential investment	5 668	5 358	5 405	5 386	5 245	5 627	6 153	7 479	8 277
Residential investment	813	865	788	801	829	929	1 011	1 232	1 408
Increase in stocks	349	473	-56	-386	-157	78	-228	-50	-193

Source: EPA, *Annual Report on National Accounts.*

151

Table I. **Local government budget (initial plan)**

Billion yen

	1985	1986	1987	1988	1989	1990	1991	1992	1993	1994	1995
General Account											
Total revenue	50 527	52 846	54 380	57 820	62 773	67 140	70 885	74 365	76 415	80 928	82 509
Local tax	22 518	24 072	24 223	26 501	28 646	30 791	32 678	34 024	34 555	32 581	33 764
Tax transfer from central government	9 912	10 314	10 557	11 126	13 932	15 600	16 615	17 563	17 386	17 428	18 139
Treasury disbursements	10 203	9 964	9 919	9 817	10 094	10 252	10 683	11 995	12 229	14 174	12 802
Local government bonds	3 950	4 429	5 390	6 048	5 559	5 624	5 611	5 140	6 225	10 392	11 305
Other	3 944	4 067	4 291	4 328	4 551	4 873	5 298	5 645	6 020	6 353	6 499
Expenditures	50 527	52 846	54 380	57 820	62 773	67 140	70 885	74 365	76 415	80 928	82 509
Salaries and pensions	14 958	15 860	16 354	16 721	17 381	18 311	19 645	20 947	21 900	22 330	22 698
General administration	10 540	11 029	11 226	11 561	12 306	12 864	13 830	14 963	15 908	16 111	16 817
Investment	16 634	17 058	17 594	19 527	20 554	21 355	22 735	24 466	26 792	29 072	30 362
Transfers to public enterprises	1 209	1 337	1 433	1 549	1 699	1 844	2 043	2 264	2 574	2 788	2 991

Source: Ministry of Finance, *Monthly Financial and Monetary Statistics (in Japanese).*

Table J. Foreign trade by commodity

$ million

	1987	1988	1989	1990	1991	1992	1993	1994
Sections:								
Exports, fob								
Food and live animals	1 425	1 568	1 546	1 482	1 607	1 655	1 676	1 668
Beverages and tobacco	121	129	141	164	215	275	331	370
Crude materials, inedible, except fuels	1 493	1 762	1 829	1 839	1 903	2 137	2 137	2 483
Mineral fuels, lubricants and related materials	783	596	972	1 283	1 323	1 625	2 005	2 326
Animal and vegetable oils and fats	85	157	83	98	81	67	63	64
Chemical products	11 665	13 967	14 782	15 879	17 483	19 125	20 234	23 669
Other manufactured goods classified chiefly by material	30 130	35 228	35 573	34 501	37 279	38 674	40 010	42 615
Machinery and transport equipment	149 598	183 781	192 179	201 311	221 205	240 935	257 748	282 754
Miscellaneous manufactured articles	31 604	24 178	24 188	25 900	28 513	29 921	30 639	32 021
Other	2 369	3 596	3 943	4 584	5 016	5 368	6 173	7 644
Total	229 273	264 960	275 236	287 040	314 625	339 781	361 017	395 614
Imports, cif								
Food and live animals	20 757	26 954	28 119	28 211	30 657	33 234	35 442	41 817
Beverages and tobacco	1 643	2 159	2 882	3 323	3 733	3 932	3 931	4 797
Crude materials, inedible, except fuels	21 745	27 631	30 224	27 952	26 659	25 307	26 736	27 760
Mineral fuels, lubricants and related materials	39 096	38 534	43 038	56 698	54 675	52 716	48 816	47 734
Animal and vegetable oils and fats	271	406	423	413	477	560	524	627
Chemical products	11 837	14 825	15 947	16 046	17 408	17 355	17 939	20 211
Other manufactured goods classified chiefly by material	18 049	27 336	30 762	30 927	31 962	26 828	28 081	32 397
Machinery and transport equipment	17 263	24 720	29 894	37 859	39 445	39 321	42 752	54 646
Miscellaneous manufactured articles	13 393	18 702	23 733	26 998	25 861	28 146	31 308	38 066
Other	5 375	6 230	5 765	6 165	5 494	5 352	5 072	6 346
Total	149 429	187 498	210 788	234 591	236 371	232 749	240 599	274 400

Source: OECD, *Monthly Statistics of Foreign Trade, Series A.*

Table K. Foreign trade by area
Monthly averages, $ million

	1985	1986	1987	1988	1989	1990	1991	1992	1993	1994
Exports, fob										
Total	14 766	17 562	19 273	22 079	22 931	23 912	26 210	28 304	30 076	32 968
OECD countries	8 698	11 074	12 057	13 539	14 022	14 282	14 898	15 650	15 883	17 054
EEC¹	1 945	2 848	3 536	4 355	4 417	4 881	5 338	5 587	4 991	5 111
North America	5 937	7 290	7 555	8 059	8 377	8 135	8 278	8 637	9 393	10 383
Australia	453	439	433	557	650	575	541	587	641	727
Other	364	497	533	568	578	691	740	840	858	833
Non-OECD countries	6 068	6 489	7 215	8 539	8 909	9 631	11 313	12 654	14 193	15 913
COMECOM	305	353	284	339	324	292	263	202	111	109
OPEC	1 049	828	694	790	710	511	716	996	1 439	1 557
Other	4 714	5 308	6 237	7 410	7 875	8 828	10 333	11 456	12 643	14 248
of which: South East Asia	2 771	3 482	4 415	5 592	6 126	6 893	8 015	8 698	9 785	11 533
Imports, cif										
Total	10 877	10 629	12 585	15 614	17 571	19 567	19 728	19 418	20 056	22 888
OECD countries	4 473	5 187	6 000	7 895	8 958	9 994	9 779	9 476	9 645	11 024
EEC¹	855	1 279	1 613	2 178	2 541	3 136	2 865	2 808	2 744	3 241
North America	2 575	2 868	3 178	4 217	4 768	5 098	5 125	5 030	5 317	6 004
Australia	626	587	662	857	967	1 031	1 084	1 037	1 018	1 133
Other	416	454	547	643	681	728	704	601	566	646
Non-OECD countries	6 404	5 442	6 585	7 720	8 613	9 573	9 949	9 942	10 410	11 864
COMECOM	155	209	255	309	348	388	396	343	139	162
OPEC	544	475	623	822	929	1 004	1 185	1 413	1 714	2 297
Other	5 704	4 758	5 706	6 588	7 336	8 181	8 368	8 187	8 558	9 404
of which: South East Asia	2 522	2 457	3 219	3 983	4 409	4 550	4 901	4 793	5 049	5 655

1. Including Portugal and Spain from 1986.
Note: Detail may not be add due to rounding.
Source: Ministry of Finance, *Summary Report on Trade of Japan;* OECD, *Monthly Statistics of Foreign Trade.*

Table N. **Public sector**

A. Budget indicators: general government accounts (per cent of GNP)[1]

	1970	1980	1985	1993
	Fiscal years			
Non-interest current receipts	20.2	26.1	28.3	29.5
Non-interest expenditure	13.7	21.9	22.1	23.1
Primary budget balance	6.6	4.2	6.2	6.4
Net interest payments[2]	–0.3	1.3	1.9	0.1
General government saving	6.9	2.9	4.3	6.3
General government net lending	1.8	–4.0	–0.8	–1.1
of which:				
Central	0.0	–5.4	–3.6	–2.9
Local	–0.4	–1.3	–0.3	–1.7
Social Security Fund	2.2	2.6	3.1	3.5
	Calendar years			
General government debt				
Gross debt	12.1	52.0	68.5	75.9
of which: Central	8.0	39.2	53.7	59.4
Net debt[3]	–6.5	17.3	26.6	4.8
of which: Central	2.0	27.1	41.0	34.0

B. The structure of general government expenditure and taxation (per cent of GNP)

	1970	1980	1985	1993
	Fiscal years			
Total expenditure				
Current consumption	7.5	9.8	9.5	9.6
Transfers to persons	4.7	10.2	11.0	12.2
Subsidies	1.2	1.5	1.1	0.7
Net interest payments[2]	–0.3	1.3	1.9	0.1
Capital formation	5.2	7.1	5.6	6.3
Total expenditure by function				
Education	3.5	4.8	4.1	3.8
Economic services[4]	4.9	5.8	4.8	5.0
Health	3.0	4.5	4.7	5.3
Housing	1.4	2.4	2.0	2.9
Social security	2.7	7.0	7.7	8.8
Total tax revenue	20.0	25.9	28.1	29.3
Direct tax	8.5	11.1	12.3	11.4
of which:				
Personal	4.1	6.3	6.8	7.5
Corporate	4.4	4.8	5.4	4.0
Social security	4.4	7.4	8.4	9.9
Indirect tax	7.2	7.4	7.5	8.0
Tax rates (per cent)				
National personal income tax				
Lowest/top rate	10/75	10/75	10.5/70	10/50
Number of brackets	19	19	15	5
General consumption tax	–	–	–	3.0

1. National accounts basis.
2. Positive sign means net expenditure.
3. Corporate shares are excluded from financial assets.
4. Includes transportation and infrastructure.
Source: Economic Planning Agency, *Annual Report on National Accounts*, Ministry of Finance, OECD, *Revenue Statistics.*

Table O. **Financial markets**

	1970	1980	1985	1993
Size of the financial sector (percentages)[1]				
Sector employment/total employment	2.4	3.0	3.2	3.4
Financial assets/GNP	159.8	228.0	291.6	372.2
Structure of financial assets and liabilities				
Financial institutions' share in domestic financial assets				
(per cent)	39.5	41.9	44.0	45.4
Net worth (per cent of GNP)				
Total	405.1	558.1	571.4	681.2
Public sector	58.1	71.7	57.2	92.9
Private sector	346.9	486.4	514.2	588.3
of which: Households	250.2	356.5	384.7	454.9
Financial assets, net (per cent of GNP)[2]				
Total	40.6	53.4	89.0	105.8
Public sector	−9.9	−39.4	−49.2	−24.9
Private sector	50.5	92.8	138.2	130.7
of which: Households	60.9	87.8	113.0	144.8

1. Financial institutions and insurance.
2. Financial assets (including corporate shares at market prices) less financial liabilities (excluding corporate shares).
Source: Economic Planning Agency, *Annual Report on National Accounts.*

Table P. Labour market indicators

A. Labour force performance

	Cyclical peak: 1985	Cyclical trough: 1986	1992	1993	1994
Unemployment rate:					
Total	2.6	2.8	2.2	2.5	2.9
Male	2.6	2.7	2.1	2.4	2.8
Female	2.7	2.8	2.2	2.6	3.0
Youth [1]	4.8	5.2	4.5	5.1	5.4
Share of long-term unemployment in total unemployment [2]	13.1	17.2	15.3	15.3	16.5
Dispersion of regional unemployment rates [3]	0.83	0.74	0.46	0.47	0.54

B. Structural or institutional characteristics

	1970	1980	1985	1994
Participation rate: [4]				
Total	65.4	63.3	63.0	63.6
Male	81.8	79.8	78.1	77.8
Female	49.9	47.6	48.7	50.2
Total employment/population (15 years and over)	64.6	62.0	61.4	61.8
Employees/total employment	64.9	71.7	74.3	81.1
Part-time employment (as per cent of employees)	7.1	10.1	11.2	18.6
Non-wage labour costs [5] (as percentage of total compensation)	8.3	11.0	13.0	14.0
Government unemployment insurance replacement ratio [6]	60/62	60/80	60/80	60/80
Unionisation rate	35.4	30.8	28.9	24.1
of which:				
Private sector	–	24.7	24.4	21.2
Public sector	–	74.5	61.7	62.5
Annual hours worked per employee	2239	2108	2110	1904

	1970/1960	1980/1970	1990/1980	1994/1993
Percentage changes (average annual rates)				
Labour force	1.4	0.9	1.2	0.5
Employment:				
Total	1.4	0.8	1.2	0.0
Primary sector	–4.1	–4.2	–2.4	–2.6
Secondary sector	3.7	0.7	0.9	–0.9
Tertiary sector	2.7	2.3	2.0	0.8

1. Unemployed persons between 15 and 24 years as a percentage of the labour force of the same age group.
2. People looking for a job since one year or more.
3. Measured by standard deviation for 10 regions.
4. Labour force as a percentage of relevant population group, aged 15 years and over.
5. Employers' contribution to social security, pension funds and others on National Accounts basis. The latest figure is for 1992.
6. Unemployment benefits per unemployed divided by the compensation per employee. Minimum and maximum ratios are shown.

Source: Management and Coordination Agency, *Labour Force Survey, Report on Special Survey of the Labour Force Survey*; Ministry of Labour, *Monthly Labour Survey, Basis Survey on Labour Unions, Monthly Labour Statistics*; Economic Planning Agency, *Annual Report on National Accounts*.

Table Q. Production structure and performance indicators

A. Production structure

	Per cent share of GDP at current market prices [1]			Per cent share of total employment		
	1970	1980	1993	1970	1980	1993
Agriculture	5.9	3.6	2.1	19.7	12.9	8.0
Mining and quarrying	0.8	0.5	0.3	0.5	0.3	0.1
Manufacturing	34.8	28.2	25.8	26.7	24.0	23.1
of which:						
Food [2]	3.7	3.2	3.1	2.5	2.4	2.5
Textiles	1.9	1.0	0.5	3.3	2.1	1.5
Chemicals and chemical products [3]	2.9	2.2	2.1	1.0	0.8	0.8
Primary metal industries	3.9	3.6	1.8	1.2	1.0	0.9
Fabricated metal products [4]	2.1	1.3	1.7	2.3	2.0	1.7
General machinery	3.7	3.0	2.9	2.9	2.5	2.7
Electrical and electronic products	3.8	3.1	3.7	2.9	2.8	3.7
Transportation equipment	3.8	3.2	2.7	2.4	2.4	2.3
Construction	7.5	9.0	9.9	8.1	10.1	9.6
Market services	43.9	48.7	52.3	37.8	44.2	50.8
of which:						
Electricity, gas and water	2.1	2.6	2.8	0.5	0.6	0.6
Wholesale and retail trade	13.9	14.8	12.1	16.0	17.8	17.4
Finance and insurance	4.1	5.0	4.2	2.4	3.0	3.4
Real estate	7.8	9.1	11.4	0.6	1.0	1.3
Transport and communications	6.7	5.9	6.1	5.5	5.7	5.6
Community, business, social and personal services	9.3	11.3	15.8	12.7	16.1	22.6
Non-market services	7.1	9.9	9.6	7.2	8.6	8.3
Government services	6.1	8.2	7.6	5.8	6.7	5.9
Community and personal services	1.0	1.7	2.0	1.4	2.0	2.4

B. Manufacturing sector performance

	Productivity growth by sector, real GDP/employment (annual rate)	
	$\dfrac{1980}{1970}$	$\dfrac{1993}{1980}$
Food [2]	3.3	−0.7
Textiles	5.8	−0.1
Chemicals and chemical products [3]	12.9	8.6
Primary metal industries	7.3	−1.0
Fabricated metal products [4]	2.9	6.1
General machinery	7.4	3.3
Electrical and electronic products	26.8	9.5
Transportation equipment	5.0	3.5

1. GDP without the adjustment for import tax, imputed interest and general consumption tax is used.
2. Excluding tobacco.
3. Excluding rubber and plastic products.
4. Excluding machinery.
Source: Economic Planning Agency, *Annual Report on National Accounts.*

BASIC STATISTICS:

INTERNATIONAL COMPARISONS

	Units	Reference period [1]	Australia	Austria
Population				
Total	Thousands	1992	17 489	7 884
Inhabitants per sq. km	Number	1992	2	94
Net average annual increase over previous 10 years	%	1992	1.4	0.4
Employment				
Civilian employment (CE) [2]	Thousands	1992	7 637	3 546
Of which: Agriculture	% of CE		5.3	7.1
Industry	% of CE		23.8	35.0
Services	% of CE		71	57.4
Gross domestic product (GDP)				
At current prices and current exchange rates	Bill. US$	1992	296.6	186.2
Per capita	US$		16 959	23 616
At current prices using current PPPs [3]	Bill. US$	1992	294.5	142
Per capita	US$		16 800	18 017
Average annual volume growth over previous 5 years	%	1992	2	3.4
Gross fixed capital formation (GFCF)	% of GDP	1992	19.7	25
Of which: Machinery and equipment	% of GDP		9.3	9.9
Residential construction	% of GDP		5.1	5.7
Average annual volume growth over previous 5 years	%	1992	−1	5.1
Gross saving ratio [4]	% of GDP	1992	15.6	25.1
General government				
Current expenditure on goods and services	% of GDP	1992	18.5	18.4
Current disbursements [5]	% of GDP	1992	36.9	46.2
Current receipts	% of GDP	1992	33.1	48.3
Net official development assistance	% of GNP	1992	0.33	0.3
Indicators of living standards				
Private consumption per capita using current PPPs [3]	US$	1992	10 527	9 951
Passenger cars, per 1 000 inhabitants	Number	1990	430	382
Telephones, per 1 000 inhabitants	Number	1990	448	589
Television sets, per 1 000 inhabitants	Number	1989	484	475
Doctors, per 1 000 inhabitants	Number	1991	2	2.1
Infant mortality per 1 000 live births	Number	1991	7.1	7.4
Wages and prices (average annual increase over previous 5 years)				
Wages (earnings or rates according to availability)	%	1992	5	5.4
Consumer prices	%	1992	5.2	3
Foreign trade				
Exports of goods, fob*	Mill. US$	1992	42 844	44 361
As % of GDP	%		14.4	23.8
Average annual increase over previous 5 years	%		10.1	10.4
Imports of goods, cif*	Mill. US$	1992	40 751	54 038
As % of GDP	%		13.7	29
Average annual increase over previous 5 years	%		8.6	10.7
Total official reserves [6]	Mill. SDRs	1992	8 152	9 006
As ratio of average monthly imports of goods	Ratio		2.4	2

* At current prices and exchange rates.
1. Unless otherwise stated.
2. According to the definitions used in OECD *Labour Force Statistics.*
3. PPPs = Purchasing Power Parities.
4. Gross saving = Gross national disposable income minus private and government consumption.
5. Current disbursements = Current expenditure on goods and services plus current transfers and payments of property income.
6. Gold included in reserves is valued at 35 SDRs per ounce. End of year.
7. Including Luxembourg.

EMPLOYMENT OPPORTUNITIES

Economics Department, OECD

The Economics Department of the OECD offers challenging and rewarding opportunities to economists interested in applied policy analysis in an international environment. The Department's concerns extend across the entire field of economic policy analysis, both macroeconomic and microeconomic. Its main task is to provide, for discussion by committees of senior officials from Member countries, documents and papers dealing with current policy concerns. Within this programme of work, three major responsibilities are:

- to prepare regular surveys of the economies of individual Member countries;
- to issue full twice-yearly reviews of the economic situation and prospects of the OECD countries in the context of world economic trends;
- to analyse specific policy issues in a medium-term context for the OECD as a whole, and to a lesser extent for the non-OECD countries.

The documents prepared for these purposes, together with much of the Department's other economic work, appear in published form in the *OECD Economic Outlook, OECD Economic Surveys, OECD Economic Studies* and the Department's *Working Papers* series.

The Department maintains a world econometric model, INTERLINK, which plays an important role in the preparation of the policy analyses and twice-yearly projections. The availability of extensive cross-country data bases and good computer resources facilitates comparative empirical analysis, much of which is incorporated into the model.

The Department is made up of about 80 professional economists from a variety of backgrounds and Member countries. Most projects are carried out by small teams and last from four to eighteen months. Within the Department, ideas and points of view are widely discussed; there is a lively professional interchange, and all professional staff have the opportunity to contribute actively to the programme of work.

Skills the Economics Department is looking for:

a) Solid competence in using the tools of both microeconomic and macroeconomic theory to answer policy questions. Experience indicates that this normally requires the equivalent of a Ph.D. in economics or substantial relevant professional experience to compensate for a lower degree.

b) Solid knowledge of economic statistics and quantitative methods; this includes how to identify data, estimate structural relationships, apply basic techniques of time series analysis, and test hypotheses. It is essential to be able to interpret results sensibly in an economic policy context.

c) A keen interest in and extensive knowledge of policy issues, economic developments and their political/social contexts.

d) Interest and experience in analysing questions posed by policy-makers and presenting the results to them effectively and judiciously. Thus, work experience in government agencies or policy research institutions is an advantage.

e) The ability to write clearly, effectively, and to the point. The OECD is a bilingual organisation with French and English as the official languages. Candidates must have excellent knowledge of one of these languages, and some knowledge of the other. Knowledge of other languages might also be an advantage for certain posts.

f) For some posts, expertise in a particular area may be important, but a successful candidate is expected to be able to work on a broader range of topics relevant to the work of the Department. Thus, except in rare cases, the Department does not recruit narrow specialists.

g) The Department works on a tight time schedule with strict deadlines. Moreover, much of the work in the Department is carried out in small groups. Thus, the ability to work with other economists from a variety of cultural and professional backgrounds, to supervise junior staff, and to produce work on time is important.

General information

The salary for recruits depends on educational and professional background. Positions carry a basic salary from FF 305 700 or FF 377 208 for Administrators (economists) and from FF 438 348 for Principal Administrators (senior economists). This may be supplemented by expatriation and/or family allowances, depending on nationality, residence and family situation. Initial appointments are for a fixed term of two to three years.

Vacancies are open to candidates from OECD Member countries. The Organisation seeks to maintain an appropriate balance between female and male staff and among nationals from Member countries.

For further information on employment opportunities in the Economics Department, contact:

Administrative Unit
Economics Department
OECD
2, rue André-Pascal
75775 PARIS CEDEX 16
FRANCE

E-Mail: compte.esadmin@oecd.org

Applications citing "ECSUR", together with a detailed *curriculum vitae* in English or French, should be sent to the Head of Personnel at the above address.

MAIN SALES OUTLETS OF OECD PUBLICATIONS
PRINCIPAUX POINTS DE VENTE DES PUBLICATIONS DE L'OCDE

ARGENTINA – ARGENTINE
Carlos Hirsch S.R.L.
Galería Güemes, Florida 165, 4° Piso
1333 Buenos Aires   Tel. (1) 331.1787 y 331.2391
Telefax: (1) 331.1787

AUSTRALIA – AUSTRALIE
D.A. Information Services
648 Whitehorse Road, P.O.B 163
Mitcham, Victoria 3132   Tel. (03) 9873.4411
Telefax: (03) 9873.5679

AUSTRIA – AUTRICHE
Gerold & Co.
Graben 31
Wien I   Tel. (0222) 533.50.14
Telefax: (0222) 512.47.31.29

BELGIUM – BELGIQUE
Jean De Lannoy
Avenue du Roi 202 Koningslaan
B-1060 Bruxelles   Tel. (02) 538.51.69/538.08.41
Telefax: (02) 538.08.41

CANADA
Renouf Publishing Company Ltd.
1294 Algoma Road
Ottawa, ON K1B 3W8   Tel. (613) 741.4333
Telefax: (613) 741.5439
Stores:
61 Sparks Street
Ottawa, ON K1P 5R1   Tel. (613) 238.8985
211 Yonge Street
Toronto, ON M5B 1M4   Tel. (416) 363.3171
Telefax: (416)363.59.63

Les Éditions La Liberté Inc.
3020 Chemin Sainte-Foy
Sainte-Foy, PQ G1X 3V6   Tel. (418) 658.3763
Telefax: (418) 658.3763

Federal Publications Inc.
165 University Avenue, Suite 701
Toronto, ON M5H 3B8   Tel. (416) 860.1611
Telefax: (416) 860.1608

Les Publications Fédérales
1185 Université
Montréal, QC H3B 3A7   Tel. (514) 954.1633
Telefax: (514) 954.1635

CHINA – CHINE
China National Publications Import ·
Export Corporation (CNPIEC)
16 Gongti E. Road, Chaoyang District
P.O. Box 88 or 50
Beijing 100704 PR   Tel. (01) 506.6688
Telefax: (01) 506.3101

CHINESE TAIPEI – TAIPEI CHINOIS
Good Faith Worldwide Int'l. Co. Ltd.
9th Floor, No. 118, Sec. 2
Chung Hsiao E. Road
Taipei   Tel. (02) 391.7396/391.7397
Telefax: (02) 394.9176

CZECH REPUBLIC – RÉPUBLIQUE TCHÈQUE
Artia Pegas Press Ltd.
Narodni Trida 25
POB 825
111 21 Praha 1   Tel. (2) 2 46 04
Telefax: (2) 2 78 72

DENMARK – DANEMARK
Munksgaard Book and Subscription Service
35, Nørre Søgade, P.O. Box 2148
DK-1016 København K   Tel. (33) 12.85.70
Telefax: (33) 12.93.87

EGYPT – ÉGYPTE
Middle East Observer
41 Sherif Street
Cairo   Tel. 392.6919
Telefax: 360-6804

FINLAND – FINLANDE
Akateeminen Kirjakauppa
Keskuskatu 1, P.O. Box 128
00100 Helsinki
Subscription Services/Agence d'abonnements :
P.O. Box 23
00371 Helsinki   Tel. (358 0) 121 4416
Telefax: (358 0) 121.4450

FRANCE
OECD/OCDE
Mail Orders/Commandes par correspondance:
2, rue André-Pascal
75775 Paris Cedex 16   Tel. (33-1) 45.24.82.00
Tel. (33-1) 49.10.42.76
Telex: 640048 OCDE
Internet: Compte.PUBSINQ @ oecd.org
Orders via Minitel, France only/
Commandes par Minitel, France exclusivement :
36 15 OCDE
OECD Bookshop/Librairie de l'OCDE :
33, rue Octave-Feuillet
75016 Paris   Tel. (33-1) 45.24.81.81
(33-1) 45.24.81.67
Dawson
B.P. 40
91121 Palaiseau Cedex   Tel. 69.10.47.00
Telefax : 64.54.83.26
Documentation Française
29, quai Voltaire
75007 Paris   Tel. 40.15.70.00
Economica
49 rue Héricart
75015 Paris   Tel. 45.78.12.92
Telefax : 40.58.15.70
Gibert Jeune (Droit-Économie)
6, place Saint-Michel
75006 Paris   Tel. 43.25.91.19
Librairie du Commerce International
10, avenue d'Iéna
75016 Paris   Tel. 40.73.34.60
Librairie Dunod
Université Paris-Dauphine
Place du Maréchal de Lattre de Tassigny
75016 Paris   Tel. 44.05.40.13
Librairie Lavoisier
11, rue Lavoisier
75008 Paris   Tel. 42.65.39.95
Librairie des Sciences Politiques
30, rue Saint-Guillaume
75007 Paris   Tel. 45.48.36.02
P.U.F.
49, boulevard Saint-Michel
75005 Paris   Tel. 43.25.83.40
Librairie de l'Université
12a, rue Nazareth
13100 Aix-en-Provence   Tel. (16) 42.26.18.08
Documentation Française
165, rue Garibaldi
69003 Lyon   Tel. (16) 78.63.32.23
Librairie Decitre
29, place Bellecour
69002 Lyon   Tel. (16) 72.40.54.54
Librairie Sauramps
Le Triangle
34967 Montpellier Cedex 2 Tel. (16) 67.58.85.15
Tekefax: (16) 67.58.27.36
A la Sorbonne Actual
23 rue de l'Hôtel des Postes
06000 Nice   Tel. (16) 93.13.77.75
Telefax: (16) 93.80.75.69

GERMANY – ALLEMAGNE
OECD Publications and Information Centre
August-Bebel-Allee 6
D-53175 Bonn   Tel. (0228) 959.120
Telefax: (0228) 959.12.17

GREECE – GRÈCE
Librairie Kauffmann
Mavrokordatou 9
106 78 Athens   Tel. (01) 32.55.321
Telefax: (01) 32.30.320

HONG-KONG
Swindon Book Co. Ltd.
Astoria Bldg. 3F
34 Ashley Road, Tsimshatsui
Kowloon, Hong Kong   Tel. 2376.2062
Telefax: 2376.0685

HUNGARY – HONGRIE
Euro Info Service
Margitsziget, Európa Ház
1138 Budapest   Tel. (1) 111.62.16
Telefax: (1) 111.60.61

ICELAND – ISLANDE
Mál Mog Menning
Laugavegi 18, Pósthólf 392
121 Reykjavik   Tel. (1) 552.4240
Telefax: (1) 562.3523

INDIA – INDE
Oxford Book and Stationery Co.
Scindia House
New Delhi 110001   Tel. (11) 331.5896/5308
Telefax: (11) 332.5993
17 Park Street
Calcutta 700016   Tel. 240832

INDONESIA – INDONÉSIE
Pdii-Lipi
P.O. Box 4298
Jakarta 12042   Tel. (21) 573.34.67
Telefax: (21) 573.34.67

IRELAND – IRLANDE
Government Supplies Agency
Publications Section
4/5 Harcourt Road
Dublin 2   Tel. 661.31.11
Telefax: 475.27.60

ISRAEL
Praedicta
5 Shatner Street
P.O. Box 34030
Jerusalem 91430   Tel. (2) 52.84.90/1/2
Telefax: (2) 52.84.93
R.O.Y. International
P.O. Box 13056
Tel Aviv 61130   Tel. (3) 546 1423
Telefax: (3) 546 1442
Palestinian Authority/Middle East:
INDEX Information Services
P.O.B. 19502
Jerusalem   Tel. (2) 27.12.19
Telefax: (2) 27.16.34

ITALY – ITALIE
Libreria Commissionaria Sansoni
Via Duca di Calabria 1/1
50125 Firenze   Tel. (055) 64.54.15
Telefax: (055) 64.12.57
Via Bartolini 29
20155 Milano   Tel. (02) 36.50.83
Editrice e Libreria Herder
Piazza Montecitorio 120
00186 Roma   Tel. 679.46.28
Telefax: 678.47.51

Libreria Hoepli
Via Hoepli 5
20121 Milano   Tel. (02) 86.54.46
                                Telefax: (02) 805.28.86

Libreria Scientifica
Dott. Lucio de Biasio 'Aeiou'
Via Coronelli, 6
20146 Milano   Tel. (02) 48.95.45.52
                                Telefax: (02) 48.95.45.48

JAPAN – JAPON
OECD Publications and Information Centre
Landic Akasaka Building
2-3-4 Akasaka, Minato-ku
Tokyo 107   Tel. (81.3) 3586.2016
                                Telefax: (81.3) 3584.7929

KOREA – CORÉE
Kyobo Book Centre Co. Ltd.
P.O. Box 1658, Kwang Hwa Moon
Seoul   Tel. 730.78.91
                                Telefax: 735.00.30

MALAYSIA – MALAISIE
University of Malaya Bookshop
University of Malaya
P.O. Box 1127, Jalan Pantai Baru
59700 Kuala Lumpur
Malaysia   Tel. 756.5000/756.5425
                                Telefax: 756.3246

MEXICO – MEXIQUE
OECD Publications and Information Centre
Edificio INFOTEC
Av. San Fernando no. 37
Col. Toriello Guerra
Tlalpan C.P. 14050
Mexico D.F.
                  Tel. (525) 606 00 11 Extension 100
                           Fax : (525) 606 13 07

Revistas y Periodicos Internacionales S.A. de C.V.
Florencia 57 - 1004
Mexico, D.F. 06600   Tel. 207.81.00
                                Telefax: 208.39.79

NETHERLANDS – PAYS-BAS
SDU Uitgeverij Plantijnstraat
Externe Fondsen
Postbus 20014
2500 EA's-Gravenhage   Tel. (070) 37.89.880
Voor bestellingen: Telefax: (070) 34.75.778

NEW ZEALAND
NOUVELLE-ZÉLANDE
GPLegislation Services
P.O. Box 12418
Thorndon, Wellington   Tel. (04) 496.5655
                                Telefax: (04) 496.5698

NORWAY – NORVÈGE
Narvesen Info Center – NIC
Bertrand Narvesens vei 2
P.O. Box 6125 Etterstad
0602 Oslo 6   Tel. (022) 57.33.00
                                Telefax: (022) 68.19.01

PAKISTAN
Mirza Book Agency
65 Shahrah Quaid-E-Azam
Lahore 54000   Tel. (42) 353.601
                                Telefax: (42) 231.730

PHILIPPINE – PHILIPPINES
International Booksource Center Inc.
Rm 179/920 Cityland 10 Condo Tower 2
HV dela Costa Ext cor Valero St.
Makati Metro Manila   Tel. (632) 817 9676
                                Telefax : (632) 817 1741

POLAND – POLOGNE
Ars Polona
00-950 Warszawa
Krakowskie Przedmieácie 7   Tel. (22) 264760
                                Telefax : (22) 268673

PORTUGAL
Livraria Portugal
Rua do Carmo 70-74
Apart. 2681
1200 Lisboa   Tel. (01) 347.49.82/5
                                Telefax: (01) 347.02.64

SINGAPORE – SINGAPOUR
Gower Asia Pacific Pte Ltd.
Golden Wheel Building
41, Kallang Pudding Road, No. 04-03
Singapore 1334   Tel. 741.5166
                                Telefax: 742.9356

SPAIN – ESPAGNE
Mundi-Prensa Libros S.A.
Castelló 37, Apartado 1223
Madrid 28001   Tel. (91) 431.33.99
                                Telefax: (91) 575.39.98

Mundi-Prensa Barcelona
Consell de Cent No. 391
08009 – Barcelona   Tel. (93) 488.34.92
                                Telefax: (93) 487.76.59

Llibreria de la Generalitat
Palau Moja
Rambla dels Estudis, 118
08002 – Barcelona
                  (Subscripcions) Tel. (93) 318.80.12
                  (Publicacions) Tel. (93) 302.67.23
                                Telefax: (93) 412.18.54

SRI LANKA
Centre for Policy Research
c/o Colombo Agencies Ltd.
No. 300-304, Galle Road
Colombo 3   Tel. (1) 574240, 573551-2
                            Telefax: (1) 575394, 510711

SWEDEN – SUÈDE
CE Fritzes AB
S–106 47 Stockholm   Tel. (08) 690.90.90
                                Telefax: (08) 20.50.21

Subscription Agency/Agence d'abonnements :
Wennergren-Williams Info AB
P.O. Box 1305
171 25 Solna   Tel. (08) 705.97.50
                                Telefax: (08) 27.00.71

SWITZERLAND – SUISSE
Maditec S.A. (Books and Periodicals - Livres
et périodiques)
Chemin des Palettes 4
Case postale 266
1020 Renens VD 1   Tel. (021) 635.08.65
                                Telefax: (021) 635.07.80

Librairie Payot S.A.
4, place Pépinet
CP 3212
1002 Lausanne   Tel. (021) 320.25.11
                                Telefax: (021) 320.25.14

Librairie Unilivres
6, rue de Candolle
1205 Genève   Tel. (022) 320.26.23
                                Telefax: (022) 329.73.18

Subscription Agency/Agence d'abonnements :
Dynapresse Marketing S.A.
38 avenue Vibert
1227 Carouge   Tel. (022) 308.07.89
                                Telefax: (022) 308.07.99

See also – Voir aussi :
OECD Publications and Information Centre
August-Bebel-Allee 6
D-53175 Bonn (Germany)   Tel. (0228) 959.120
                                Telefax: (0228) 959.12.17

THAILAND – THAÏLANDE
Suksit Siam Co. Ltd.
113, 115 Fuang Nakhon Rd.
Opp. Wat Rajbopith
Bangkok 10200   Tel. (662) 225.9531/2
                                Telefax: (662) 222.5188

TURKEY – TURQUIE
Kültür Yayinlari Is-Türk Ltd. Sti.
Atatürk Bulvari No. 191/Kat 13
Kavaklidere/Ankara   Tel. 428.11.40 Ext. 2458
Dolmabahce Cad. No. 29
Besiktas/Istanbul   Tel. (312) 260 7188
                                Telex: (312) 418 29 46

UNITED KINGDOM – ROYAUME-UNI
HMSO
Gen. enquiries   Tel. (171) 873 8496
Postal orders only:
P.O. Box 276, London SW8 5DT
Personal Callers HMSO Bookshop
49 High Holborn, London WC1V 6HB
                                Telefax: (171) 873 8416
Branches at: Belfast, Birmingham, Bristol,
Edinburgh, Manchester

UNITED STATES – ÉTATS-UNIS
OECD Publications and Information Center
2001 L Street N.W., Suite 650
Washington, D.C. 20036-4910 Tel. (202) 785.6323
                                Telefax: (202) 785.0350

VENEZUELA
Libreria del Este
Avda F. Miranda 52, Aptdo. 60337
Edificio Galipán
Caracas 106   Tel. 951.1705/951.2307/951.1297
                            Telegram: Libreste Caracas

Subscriptions to OECD periodicals may also be
placed through main subscription agencies.

Les abonnements aux publications périodiques de
l'OCDE peuvent être souscrits auprès des
principales agences d'abonnement.

Orders and inquiries from countries where Distributors have not yet been appointed should be sent to:
OECD Publications Service, 2 rue André-Pascal,
75775 Paris Cedex 16, France.

Les commandes provenant de pays où l'OCDE n'a
pas encore désigné de distributeur peuvent être
adressées à : OCDE, Service des Publications,
2, rue André-Pascal, 75775 Paris Cedex 16, France.

10-1995

OECD PUBLICATIONS, 2 rue André-Pascal, 75775 PARIS CEDEX 16
PRINTED IN FRANCE
(10 95 03 1) ISBN 92-64-14668-7 - No. 48177 1995
ISSN 0376-6438